Prague

by Christopher and Melanie Rice

Since Christopher completed his PhD in Russian history, he and Melanie have travelled widely and have written numerous travel guides. Their titles for AA Publishing include *Essential Austria*, *Essential Budapest*, *CityPack Moscow*, *CityPack Istanbul*, *AA/Thomas Cook Travellers Berlin*, *Explorer Moscow and St Petersburg* and, most recently, *Explorer Turkish Coast*. The Rices first visited Prague at the time of the Velvet Revolution and have watched dev

Ab

D1470862

AA Publishing

Above: a hat seller

Written by Christopher and Melanie Rice

First published 1998
Reprinted 2001. Information verified and updated.
Reprinted Apr and Aug 2002. Reprinted Jan 2004,
May 2004.
This edition 2005. Information verified and updated.

Published by AA Publishing, a trading name of
Automobile Association Developments Limited,
whose registered office is Southwood East, Apollo
Rise, Farnborough, Hampshire, GU14 0JW.
Registered number 1878835.

A CIP catalogue record for this book is available from the
British Library.

The contents of this publication are believed correct at
the time of printing. Nevertheless, the publishers cannot
be held responsible for any errors or omissions or for
changes in the details given in this guide or for the
consequences of any reliance on the information it
provides. This does not affect your statutory rights.
Assessments of attractions, hotels, restaurants and other
sights are based upon the author's personal experience
and, therefore, necessarily contain elements of subjective
opinion which may not reflect the publisher's opinion or
dictate a reader's own experience on another occasion.

We have tried to ensure accuracy in this guide, but
things do change and we would be grateful if readers
would advise us of any inaccuracies they may encounter.

Find out more about
AA Publishing and the
wide range of travel
publications and services
the AA provides by
visiting our website at
www.theAA.com/bookshop

A01990

Colour separation: Keenes, Andover
Printed and bound in Italy by Printer Trento S.r.l.

Contents

About this Book

This book is divided into five sections to cover the most important aspects of your visit to Prague.

Viewing Prague pages 5–14
An introduction to Prague by the author
   Prague's Features
   Essence of Prague
   The Shaping of Prague
   Peace and Quiet
   Prague's Famous

Top Ten pages 15–26
The author's choice of the Top Ten places to see in Prague, each with practical information

What to See pages 27–90
Two sections: Prague and Excursions, each with its own brief introduction and an alphabetical listing of the main attractions
   Practical information
   Snippets of 'Did You Know...' information
   4 suggested walks
   2 suggested tours
   2 features

Where To... pages 91–116
Detailed listings of the best places to eat, stay, shop, take the children and be entertained.

Practical Matters pages 117–24
A highly visual section containing essential travel information.

Maps
All map references are to the individual maps found in the What to See section of this guide.
For example, Katedrála Svatého Víta has the reference ➕ 41D2 – indicating the page on which the map is located and the grid square in which the cathedral is to be found. A list of the maps that have been used in this travel guide can be found in the index.

Prices
Where appropriate, an indication of the cost of an establishment is given by **£** signs:
£££ denotes higher prices, **££** denotes average prices, while **£** denotes lower charges.

Star Ratings
Most of the places described in this book have been given a separate rating:
✪✪✪   Do not miss
✪✪   Highly recommended
✪   Worth seeing

Viewing
Prague

Above: *St John of
Nepomuk, Charles
Bridge*
Right: *studying a
map of Praha*

Christopher &
Melanie Rice's Prague

Prague Submerged
In January, 2004, 18 months after Prague suffered the worst floods in more than a century, the end of repair work was marked by an official celebration. The flash floods of August 2002 struck at the city's historic core as the River Vltava rose to ten times its normal level. The Lesser Quarter, Kampa Island and Josefov were the worst affected areas, but fortunately mela barriers kept the waters at bay in the Old Town. Even so, more that 50,000 people were forced to leave their homes and the damage to the city's infrastructure (including the metro system) was enormous.

Gregarious Czechs take time out for a game of cards in Václavské náměstí (Wenceslas Square)

Praguers know their minds and have always been willing – though not always able – to express them. Standing in Old Town Square, one is reminded of the great Czech religious reformer, Jan Hus, who took on the might of the Catholic Church in order to stand up for what he believed. As so often in the nation's history it was an unequal, albeit heroic, struggle. Over 500 years later, in January 1969, a university student, Jan Palach, suffered a horrific death by self-immolation rather than acquiesce in the Soviet invasion.

Politicians, of course, prefer to leave permanent monuments in brick and stone – the Klementinum, the Charles Bridge, the Valdštejn Palace, Obecní Dům. Everywhere you walk in Prague, its buildings are reminders of the city's history; but they are also aesthetic statements by the architects, artists and sculptors who contributed so much to this most beautiful city. Prague is much more than a glorified museum, however; it is a dynamic place, where individuals are allowed, even encouraged, to stand out from the crowd. To take the city's pulse, spend time in the pubs and cafés that poke out of every nook and cranny. For the traditional view, head for U Zlatého Tygra (➤ 115), a spit and sawdust, no-nonsense establishment where the customers set the world to rights. But just as representative of today's Prague is Radost FX (➤ 97), a meeting place for young people from all corners of the world. The growing café culture is symptomatic of the direction the city is taking. Increasingly cosmopolitan and receptive to new ideas, Prague is now more irresistible than ever.

Prague's Features

Geography
• Prague lies on the River Vltava at 50° 5' north and 14° 25' east – the heart of Central Europe. The lowest point is 176m above sea level, the highest 396m. Prague is 292km from Vienna, 350km from Berlin, 1,037km from Paris and 1,377km from London.

Climate
• Prague has a mild climate with an average yearly temperature of 9°C. Summers are moderately warm, the hottest months being July and August, when the average temperature reaches 19°C. These are also the wettest months. In January and February, the two coldest months, temperatures hover around 0°C, and there are often sharp frosts.

Population
• Prague covers an area of 497sq km, about two-thirds that of New York, but its population is only 1,178,000, compared with New York City's 8 million. Fewer than 30,000 people (2.5 per cent) live in the historic core of the city; the overwhelming majority inhabit apartment blocks known as *paneláks*, on the outskirts. Approximately 95.5 per cent of the population is of Czech nationality.

Religion
• Although there are hundreds of Roman Catholic and Protestant churches in Prague – 'the city of a thousand spires' (actually 500) – the Czechs are not a deeply religious people. In one survey less than 20 per cent admitted to a belief in God.

Tourism
• In 2003 around 10 per cent of the Czech Republic's 95 million foreign visitors spent at least part of their stay in Prague. The countries best represented were Germany, Poland, Great Britain, Italy and Slovakia – the Japanese spent the most money. Tourism in 2003 remained a major source of income, 20 per cent up on the 2002 figure.

Environment Facts and Figures
Prague has:
10,000 hectares of green space
31km of rivers, 10 islands and 18 bridges
500,000 road vehicles
2,570km of road
130km of tram lines
43km of metro line with 43 stations

Josef Schulz's magnificent Ceremonial Hall is the outstanding architectural feature of the Národní muzeum (National Museum)

Essence of Prague

It is easy to get to know Prague, even to feel at home here. To enjoy the city to the full, be prepared to abandon your sightseeing itinerary whenever the mood takes you – the galleries and museums can wait. Put away the map and wander off the beaten track. Don't neglect the side streets and courtyards, where Prague is often at its most beguiling. To see more, take the tram rather than the metro, and be prepared to go the extra mile: climb to the top of that hill – no city in Europe has more rewarding views.

Two of Prague's many beguiling faces

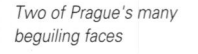

THE **10** ESSENTIALS

If you only have a short time to visit Prague, or would like to get a really complete picture of the city, here are the essentials:

• **Watch Christ and his Twelve Apostles** signal the hour as they emerge from the Astronomical Clock in Old Town Square (➤ 22).

• **Go to see Kafka's house** in Golden Lane (➤ 73), in the grounds of Prague Castle (➤ 20–1).

• **Listen to the buskers** on the Charles Bridge (➤ 40), while browsing the stalls for souvenirs.

• **Take tram 22** on its scenic journey through the Malá Strana and up to Hradčany.

Veletrzny Palace (➤ 26).

• **Listen to some Mozart** –

• **Take a walk up Wenceslas Square** (➤ 25) stopping to look at Jan Myslbek's famous equestrian statue of St Wenceslas and the small shrine to the martyrs of the Communist era.

• **Visit U Zlatého Tygra** at Jilská 4: a traditional Czech pub, where guests sit at plain wooden tables and wait to be served glasses of the frothy Pilsner Urquell lager (➤ 115).

• **See the Picassos** in the

the real thing at the Estates Theatre (➤ 70) or starring puppets at the National Marionette Theatre (➤ 112).

• **Visit the wonderful art nouveau confection, Obecní Dům** (➤ 61). Built as a civic centre in the early 1900s, it has recently been completely renovated.

• **Enjoy the peaceful surroundings** of the Royal Gardens (➤ 50).

Above: *this picturesque cottage in Zlatá ulička (Golden Lane) was once the home of the writer Franz Kafka*
Top: *café life in Staroměské náměstí (Old Town Square)*

9

The Shaping of Prague

Late 9th century
Prince Bořivoj I builds a timber fort on Hradčany.

c935
Duke Wenceslas (later patron saint of Bohemia) is murdered by his brother, Boleslav.

1085
Vratislav II is crowned first King of Bohemia by the Holy Roman Emperor, Henry IV.

1234
Founding of the Staré Město (Old Town), which is fortified with towers, walls and a moat.

1257
Otokar II invites German merchants and tradesmen to settle in the Malá

Emperor Rudolph II converses with the astronomer Johannes Kepler

Strana (Lesser Quarter).

1346–78
The reign of Charles IV, Prague's Golden Age. Work begins on St Vitus's Cathedral and the Charles Bridge. The Karolinum (Prague University) and the Nové Město (New Town) are founded.

1415
The religious reformer, Jan Hus, is burnt at the stake for heresy at the Council of Constance in Switzerland.

1419
Hussite rebels throw

several city councillors from the windows of the New Town Hall, an incident known to history as the First Defenestration of Prague.

1576–1611
Reign of Emperor Rudolph II. A man of wide and varied interests, he invites the astronomers Tycho Brahe and Johannes Kepler to the city.

1618
Second Defenestration of Prague. Several of Ferdinand II's councillors are hurled from the windows of Prague Castle, this time by Protestant noblemen. The incident triggers the Thirty Years' War.

1620
Battle of the White Mountain. Bohemia's Protestants are defeated and the Counter-Reformation triumphs.

1848
Czech nationalism is strengthened following a revolt by students and workers, which is ruthlessly suppressed by the Austrian General Windischgrätz.

1883
The National Theatre is completed and becomes the cultural focus of opposition to Hapsburg rule.

1914–18
World War I. The Czechs are dragged into the conflict on the Austrian side, although many Czech conscripts desert.

1918
With the defeat of Austria-Hungary, the new Republic of Czechoslovakia is proclaimed in Obecní Dům. Tomáš Masaryk is elected as first president.

1939
Hitler dismembers what remains of Czechoslovakia after the Munich agreement. The Nazis set up the Protectorate of Bohemia and Moravia. Prague's Jews are rounded up and sent to concentration camps.

1939–45
World War II. The German Occupation continues until 1945, when the people of Prague liberate their city and welcome the arrival of the Red Army.

1948
The Communist Party seizes power in what amounts to a *coup d'état*. Beginning of one-party rule and Stalinist repression.

1968
Prime Minister Alexander Dubček introduces the reforms known as 'The Prague Spring'. In August Soviet troops lead the Warsaw Pact invasion of Czechoslovakia.

1977
The dissident playwright, Václav Havel, is one of the founders of Charter '77, a movement protest-ing against the violation of human rights.

1989
'The Velvet Revolution'. After weeks of unrest, the Communist government resigns on 10 December and on the 29th Václav Havel is elected president.

1990
Havel's Civic Forum gains over half the seats in the first free elections.

1993
On 1 January Czechoslovakia splits into separate Czech and Slovak states. Prague becomes the capital of the Czech Republic and Havel begins a new five-year term as president.

1999
The Czechs are formally admitted to NATO.

2004
The Czech Republic joins the European Union.

Sombre memorial to the villagers of Lidice, killed by the Nazis in 1942

Peace & Quiet

In the City

Prague is fortunate in the variety and proximity of its green spaces, from the wooded hillsides of Petřín and Letná to the public gardens near Wenceslas Square. For a quiet stroll, try the banks of the Vltava at Na Kampě or the former royal hunting grounds of Stromovka (trams 5, 12, 17, 51, 53 or 54 to Holesovice). Keep to the western end (away from the exhibition centre), which was planted as early as 1593, when the lakes and ponds were laid out. The landscaped slopes leading to the Summer Palace of the Czech Governors (1805–11) are a popular spot for picnics.

Krkonoše National Park

Forested paths and peak trails are the main attraction of the Krkonoše (Giant) Mountains, 150km northwest of Prague. One of the most popular routes is along the ridge from Harrachov to Sněžka, following the Polish border. (There are year-round chair lifts to the upper slopes.) This is a good area for bird-watching: alpine accentors and water pipits can be seen on the higher ridges, nutcrackers and woodpeckers on the wooded slopes. The park's administrative centre is at Vrchlabi, but Špindlerův, Mlyn and Rec pod Snežkou are all good bases from which to explore the area.

Stromovka Park is one of Prague's most popular green spaces

Slapy Dam

The 65m-high dam across the Vltava River took four years to build and was completed in 1954. The reservoir is a favourite with Prague residents, who flock to the holiday bungalows dotted along its wooded shores to enjoy a weekend's fishing, swimming, boating and water sports. Slapy can be reached directly on route 102, south of Prague, or at a more leisurely pace, by boat (the trip up the Vltava takes four hours).

Šumava Hills

Forested with beech, fir and spruce, this beautiful area of gently rolling upland lies along the German border. Above the tree line are meadows and grasslands which flower in spring and summer. South of Sušice, a 7km nature trail leads through the scenic Vydra Valley, which can also be reached by road (route 169). Alternatively, take the 163, which follows the course of the Vltava and the impressive

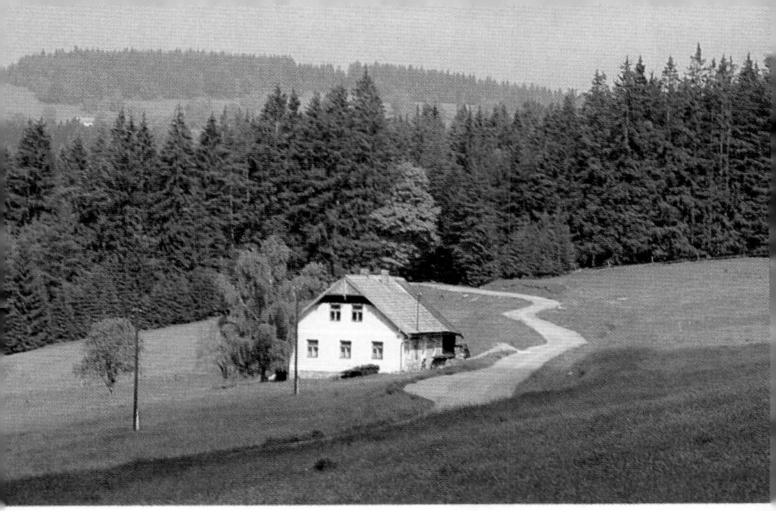

Lipno dam. From here it's a short drive (42km) north again to one of the most beautiful towns of the Czech Republic, Český Krumlov.

The Šumava Hills are an area of great scenic beauty not far from the Czech–German border

The Bohemian Karst

The Karst is a protected area, rich in rare flora – orchids flourish in the slightly acidic limestone soils. Gorges, sinkholes, caves and other unusual rock formations evolved over time due to rainwater erosion, and make for an interesting landscape. Between the castles of Karlštejn and Křivoklát is the stunning Berounka river valley, where red markers indicate rewarding forest trails.

The Bohemian Lakeland

There are more than 6,000 fish ponds in the area around Třeboň, many of them laid out in the 16th century by Štěpánek Netolicky and Mikulas Rathard, fishmasters to the Rožmberks, who owned the land. South of Třeboň is the Svět lake, where locals like to swim and go windsurfing in hot weather. The best way to enjoy the surrounding countryside is to hire a bike – the flat, marshy terrain is a rich habitat for toads and dragonflies and for water birds such as grebes, wildfowl and herons.

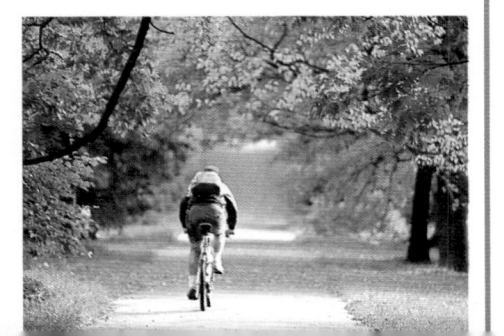

Cycling is one of the most enjoyable ways of getting to know the Czech countryside

Prague's Famous

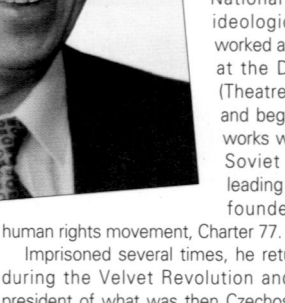

Still the face of the Czech Republic – former President Václav Havel

The Havel Connection
Václav Havel's maternal grandfather, Hugo Vavřecky, was a prominent Prague journalist and diplomat who went on to become managing director of the Bata shoe firm. His highly prized porcelain collection is exhibited at Troja Chateau. Havel's uncle, Miloš, together with Max Urban, founded the Czech film studios at Barrandov in 1933. His paternal grandfather, also called Václav, was a leading avant-garde architect who designed the Lucerna Arcade on Wenceslas Square (► 107).

Václav Havel

Playwright, essayist, former dissident and latterly statesman on the world stage, Václav Havel finally stepped down as Czech President in February 2003 after serving three consecutive terms. Born in Prague on 5 October 1936, Havel turned to the theatre in the late 1950s after being refused a place at the National Film School on ideological grounds. He worked as a lighting technician at the Divadlo Na Zábradlí (Theatre on the Balustrade) and began writing plays. His works were banned after the Soviet invasion and, as a leading dissident, he was a founder member of the human rights movement, Charter 77.

Imprisoned several times, he returned to prominence during the Velvet Revolution and was first elected president of what was then Czechoslovakia in December 1989. After leaving hospital, in January 1997, following a lung operation, the president announced he was marrying the well-known Czech actress, Dagmar Veskrnova, only a year after the death of his first wife, Olga. His approval ratings slumped but only temporarily; today he is as highly respected in his own country as he is abroad.

Franz Kafka

One of the 20th century's most influential writers, Franz Kafka was virtually unknown when he died of tuberculosis in 1924 aged 41. Born at U Radnice 5 in 1883, he lived at some 15 addresses in the city, mostly around Old Town Square, where his father owned a haberdasher's shop (Staroměstské náměstí 8). Kafka went to school at the German Gymnasium in the Kinsky Palace before receiving a doctorate in law from the Karolinum in 1906. During his student years he wrote in his spare time. His gathering obsession with bureaucratic oppression probably derives from his work as an insurance clerk. In the words of a friend, Johnnes Urzidil, Prague is 'everywhere in Kafka's work, in tiny splinters' – most famously in his short story, *Description of a Struggle*, and the nightmarish novel, *The Castle*, for which the prototype is clearly Pražský hrad.

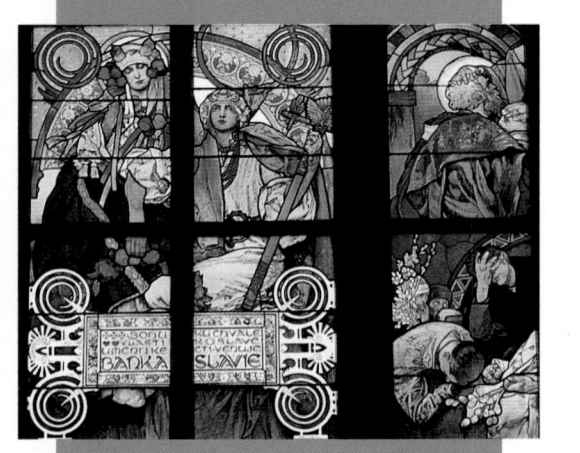

Top Ten

Above: *Katedrála Svatého Víta
stained-glass window*
Right: *gate bronzes*

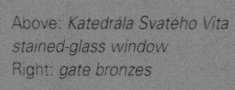

15

1
Chrám Svatého Mikuláše
(St Nicholas's Church)

www.pslaterium.cz

✚ 30B2

✉ Malostranské náměstí

☎ None

🕐 Apr–Oct daily 9–5,
Nov–Mar daily 9–4.
Belfry Apr–Oct for
concerts

🍴 Cafés (£), restaurants
(££–£££) near by

Ⓜ Malostranská

🚌 12, 22

🚊 None ♿ Few

✋ Cheap

↔ Karlův most (➤ 40),
Malostranské náměstí
(➤ 53), Valdštejnský
palác (➤ 71)

The all-powerful Jesuit Order commissioned this superb church, the ultimate expression of Prague baroque, at the beginning of the 18th century.

Recently restored at a cost of 120 million Czech crowns, this monumental building was constructed in 1704–56 by the father-and-son team, Christoph and Kilián Dientzenhofer, and completed by Kilián's son-in-law, Anselmo Lurago. The interior decoration builds on an accumulation of *trompe l'oeil* effects, culminating in *The Apotheosis of St Nicholas* by Johann Kracker, a fresco covering more than 1,500sq m of the nave ceiling. The splendid dome, by Kilián Dietzenhofer, is 18m higher than the Petřín Tower. But not everything is as costly as it appears. Many of the mottled pink and green pillars, cornices and other details, for example, are *faux marbre*, while the four more than life-size statues under the dome are made of wood, with a surface covering of glazed chalk. These dramatic characterisations of the Church Fathers include a vigorous St Cyril triumphantly lancing the devil with his crozier. The sculptor, Ignaz Platzer, also created the copper statue of St Nicholas, which looks down from the high altar. Two other features are worthy of note: the rococo pulpit, overhanging with angels and cherubs, was

Chrám Svatého Mikuláše in the Malá Strana is Prague's most extravagant baroque monument

made by Peter and Richard Práchner in 1765. The baroque organ, played by Mozart in 1787, boasts 2,500 pipes and 44 registers. Four years later it was played at a funeral mass in his memory. The church was full to overflowing, evidence of the esteem in which he was held here.

2
Josefov

For more than 700 years this attractive neighbourhood of the Old Town has been home to Prague's Jewish community.

Jews first settled in the Old Town in the 12th century. In 1254 the area was surrounded by a ghetto wall, following a decree of the third Lateran Council. The ghetto was a centre of learning, with its own Talmudic school and Hebrew printing press. Although Prague's Jews were regularly subjected to discrimination and persecution, wealthy elders, like Mayor Mordechai Maisel in the 16th century, won privileges for the ghetto by placing their wealth at the disposal of the imperial treasury. In 1784 Emperor Joseph II relaxed many restrictions, and in 1849 Josefov (as the Jewish quarter was now called) was incorporated into the city. Most of the ghetto slums were demolished at the end of the 19th century. The Holocaust all but wiped out the Jewish population of Prague – today's community numbers only about 1,000.

Hitler planned a museum in Josefov recording the history of the 'extinct' Jewish race. Ironically, this ensured the preservation of treasures and furnishings confiscated from synagogues all over Bohemia and Moravia. They are now exhibited in three of the restored synagogues. Other features include a medieval cemetery, and the Old-New Synagogue, which has been the focus of religious worship since the 13th century. Two other museums, the Pinkas Synagogue and the Ceremonial Hall, are impressive memorials to the Holocaust. The former Town Hall, dating from 1763, is a baroque building with a distinctive green steeple. Set in one of the gables is a clock with hands that travel anti-clockwise, following the Hebrew lettering, which is read from right to left.

The Hebrew clock on the roof of the Town Hall in Josefov. There has been a Jewish community in Prague for more than 800 years

www.jewishmuseum.cz

✚ 31C3

✉ Jáchymova 3, Josefov, Praha 1

☎ 2248 19458 (Jewish Museum)

🕐 Sun–Fri 9–4:30. Closed Jewish hols

🍴 Café (£), restaurant (££) near by

🚇 Staroměstská

🚌 17, 18, 135, 207

🚏 None

♿ Few

✋ Moderate

↔ Anežský klášter (► 30–1), Klausová synagóga (► 44), Maiselova synagóga (► 53), Obřadní síň (► 64), Pinkasova synagóga (► 65), Staronová synagóga (► 69), Stary židovský hřbitov (► 69)

3
Katedrála Svatého Víta
(St Vitus's Cathedral)

St Vitus's took nearly six centuries to complete and was consecrated only in 1929. Yet it stands on the site of a chapel founded in 925.

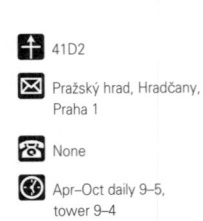

✚ 41D2

✉ Pražský hrad, Hradčany, Praha 1

☎ None

🕐 Apr–Oct daily 9–5, tower 9–4

🍴 Café (£), restaurants (££–£££) near by

Ⓜ None

🚌 22

🚊 None

♿ Few

✋ Free

↔ Pražský hrad (▶ 20–1), Klášter Svatého Jiří (▶ 43)

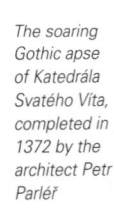

❓ Moderate charge for crypt, tower and choir

Work started on the present Gothic building in 1344, under the direction of Matthias of Arras. The German, Petr Parléř (Peter Parler), and his two sons were responsible for the lofty choir and the surrounding chapels, which were finally completed early in the 15th century. The tower on the south side was given its Renaissance steeple in 1562, to which baroque embellishments were later added. The nave and the impressive west end date from the second half of the 19th century. The Golden Portal (the original entrance), on the south side, contains a mosaic of the Last Judgement, dating from 1370, which has recently been restored to its former glory.

The Chapel of St Wenceslas, dating from 1358–67, is one of the oldest parts of the building and the most beautifully decorated. The lower walls are encrusted with scintillating jasper and amethyst, while the frescos (14th–16th centuries) depict scenes from the passion of Christ and the life of St Wenceslas (the saint is buried directly underneath the chapel). The foundations of the 11th-century Romanesque basilica were unearthed as the cathedral was nearing completion and can be seen in the crypt, along with the sarcophagi of the kings of Bohemia. King Vladislav Jagiello commissioned the beautiful Royal Oratory in the 1480s: the vaulted ceiling, shaped like the branches of a tree, is highly unusual. An exquisite silver funerary monument to the cult saint, John of Nepomuk, by Fischer von Erlach, was erected in the choir in 1736. One of the cherubs points to the saint's tongue, which was said never to have decayed. The cathedral also contains fine 20th-century stained glass, notably Alfons Mucha's portrait of saints Cyril and Methodius in the third chapel from the west end.

The soaring Gothic apse of Katedrála Svatého Víta, completed in 1372 by the architect Petr Parléř

4
Loreta

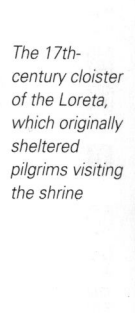

This pretty baroque shrine has been a place of pilgrimage since 1626, when it was endowed by a Bohemian noblewoman, Katežina of Lobkowicz.

The Loreta shrine was inspired by a medieval legend. In 1278, so the story goes, the Virgin Mary's house in Nazareth was miraculously transported by angels to Loreto in Italy and thus saved from the Infidel. The Marian cult became an important propaganda weapon of the Counter-Reformation and, following the defeat of the Protestants at the Battle of the White Mountain in 1620, some 50 other Loreto shrines were founded in Bohemia and Moravia.

The 17th-century cloister of the Loreta, which originally sheltered pilgrims visiting the shrine

The heart of the Loreta is the Santa Casa, a replica of the Virgin's relocated house. Sumptuously decorated, it incorporates a beam and several bricks from the Italian original. On the silver altar (behind a grille) is a small ebony statue of the Virgin. The rich stucco reliefs, depicting scenes from the lives of the prophets, are by Italian artists.

The much larger Church of the Nativity was designed by Kilian Dientzenhofer in 1734–5, with ceiling frescos by Václav Reiner and Johann Schöpf. Less edifying are the gruesome remains of saints Felecissimus and Marcia, complete with wax death masks. The cloisters, originally 17th century but with an upper storey added by Dientzenhofer in the 1740s, once provided overnight shelter for pilgrims. In the corner chapel of Our Lady of Sorrows is a diverting painting of St Starosta, a bearded lady who prayed for facial hair to put off an unwanted suitor, only to be crucified by her thwarted father. The Loreta treasury has a famed collection of vestments and other religious objects, including a diamond monstrance made in Vienna in 1699, which glitters with 6,200 precious stones.

✚ 30A3

✉ Loretánské náměstí 7, Praha 1

☎ 2205 16740

🕐 Tue–Sun 9–12:15, 1–4:30

🍴 None   🚇 None

🚌 22

🚊 None   ♿ None

💰 Moderate

↔ Strahovský klášter (► 24)

5
Pražský Hrad
(Prague Castle)

*Dominating Hradčany with majestic assurance,
Prague Castle has a history stretching back more
than a thousand years and is still the Czech State's
administrative centre.*

www.hrad.cz

✝ 30B3

✉ Hradčany, Praha 1

☎ 2243 73368

🕐 Apr–Oct daily 9–5,
Nov–Mar daily 9–4

🍴 Cafés (£), restaurants
(££–£££)

🚊 None

🚌 22

🚇 None

♿ Good

✋ Moderate

↔ Katedrála Svatého Víta
(► 18), Klášter Svatého
Jiří (► 43), Zlatá ulička
(► 73)

❓ Information Centre in
second courtyard.
Changing of the guard
every hour on the hour
at the main gate.

The Castle's château-like appearance dates from 1753–75,
when the Empress of Austria, Maria-Theresa, ordered its
reconstruction, but the Gothic towers and spires of St
Vitus's Cathedral are clues to a much older history. Sieges,
burnings, floods and other misfortunes all took their toll on
the churches and palaces, culminating in a disastrous fire
in 1541 which engulfed the whole of Hradčany.
Architecturally this was a blessing in disguise: the
extensive repairs and restoration work which went on for
more than a century, under the supervision of Italian and
native architects, resulted in the stunning Renaissance and
baroque interiors of today's Royal Palace.

Entry to the Castle is through a series of enclosed
courtyards. In the first, the changing of the guard takes
place hourly in the shadow of huge baroque sculptures of
battling Titans (the soldiers' uniforms were designed by
Theodor Pist, who fitted out the actors in the film
Amadeus). The entrance to the second courtyard is
through the Matthias Gate, which dates from 1614.
Directly opposite is the 19th-century Chapel of the Cross,
now the Information Centre. On the other side of the
courtyard, the Picture Gallery of Prague Castle contains
paintings from the Imperial collections, including minor
works by Titian, Tintoretto,
Veronese and Rubens. The
third courtyard is dominated
by St Vitus's Cathedral
(► 18). To the right, the
18th-century façade of the
Royal Palace conceals a
network of halls and
chambers on various levels,
dating from the Romanesque
period onwards. The centrepiece is the magnificent
Vladislav Hall, built for King
Vladislav Jagiello in the
1490s with Benedikt Ried's
eye-catching rib-vaulted
ceiling. Coronation feasts,
political assemblies, even
jousting competitions took
place in the hall; knights on

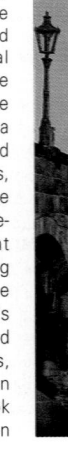

horeseback entered by the Riders' Staircase at the far end. Off to the right are the former offices of the Chancellery of Bohemia, dating from the early 16th century, where, on 23 May 1618, after learning of the accession to the throne of the detested Archduke Ferdinand of Hapsburg, more than 100 Protestant noblemen burst into the far room and threw two Catholic governors and a secretary out of the window. The officials survived the fall but the incident, known as the Defenestration of Prague, marked the start of the Thirty Years' War. The Chapel of All Saints was redecorated in baroque style after the fire of 1541, but much more impressive is the Diet Hall, next door. Once a medieval parliament and later a throne room, it was designed by the Renaissance architect, Bonifaz Wohlmut, in 1563 and its walls are hung with portraits of the Hapsburgs. The Riders' Staircase leads down to the remains of the Romanesque and Gothic Palaces and an exhibition on the castle.

The Castle complex's other outstanding monument is St George's Basilica (► 43). A short walk away is the Lobkowicz Palace, reconstructed by Carlo Lurago in the 17th century. The impressive banqueting hall is open for concerts and recitals (other rooms are used by the Museum of Czech history). Two of the Castle's towers are open to visitors. Beyond Golden Lane, the Dalibor Tower was constructed in 1496 and is named after a nobleman imprisoned here on suspicion of complicity in a peasants' revolt. In the Mihulka, or Powder Tower, alchemists were once employed to elicit the secret of turning base metals into gold.

Above: *Ignaz Platzer's* Fighting Giants *dwarf the sentries outside the First Courtyard of Pražský hrad*

Below: *looking across River Vltava to Prague Castle*

6
Staroměstská Radnice
(Old Town Hall)

31C2

Staroměstská náměstí
1, Praha 1

2360 02562

Apr–Oct Mon 11–6,
Tue–Sun 9–6, Nov–Mar
Mon 11–5, Tue–Sun 9–5

Cafés (££), restaurants
(£££) near by

Staroměstská

17

Few

Moderate

Celetná (▶ 34), Dům U
Kamenného Zvonu
(▶ 38), Kostel Panny
Marie před Týnem
(▶ 46), Kostel Sv
Mikuláše (▶ 48),
Muzeum Českého Skla
(▶ 55), Staroměstská
náměstí (▶ 68)

Guided tours available.
Tourist information
office open all year
round

*The star attraction of Prague's most famous
landmark is the enchanting Astronomical Clock.*

The Old Town Hall is actually a row of houses, adapted by
the council over the centuries. In 1338 the burghers
enlarged the merchant Volflin's house, and the adjoining
tower and chapel were added in 1381. All that remains of
the original façade is the door, with superb wood carvings
by Matthias Rejsek. Neighbouring Kříž House was acquired
six years later – the Rennaisance window, inscribed *Praga
caput regni* (Prague, capital of the kingdom), is 16th-
century. The house of furrier Mikš was added in 1548 and
the house At the Cock in the 19th century.

The delicate mechanisms of the Astronomical Clock
contrive to give the time of day, the months and seasons
of the year, the signs of the zodiac, the course of the sun
and the holidays of the Christian calendar. On the stroke of
the hour, death, in the form of a skeleton, tolls a bell
before making way for the 12 Apostles. When the cock
crows and the clock chimes, other figures appear,
including an infidel Turk and a preening Vanity.

Part of the Town Hall is open to the public. The council
chamber has a fine casetto ceiling (1470). The oriel chapel,
designed by Petr Parléř, also has a magnificent ceiling,
painted with frescos of the four evangelists against an
azure blue background with golden stars. Climb the tower
for unsurpassed views across the red rooftops of the city.

*The Astronomical Clock is
one of the most appealing
attractions in
Staroměstské náměstí
(Old Town Square)*

7

Šternberský Palác
(Sternberg Palace)

The 17th-century baroque palace, built for Count Wenceslas Sternberg in 1698–1707, now houses the National Gallery's impressive collection of Old Masters.

The palace is set back from Hradčany Square (▶ 40): access is through the left-hand entrance of the Archbishop's Palace. The exhibition is arranged chronologically by the artists' country of origin. The gallery's proudest possession is Albrecht Dürer's scintillating *Feast of the Rose Garlands* (1506), acquired by Emperor Rudolph II because it features one of his ancestors, Maximilian I (shown in the foreground with Pope Julius II). German painting is also represented by Holbein the Elder and Lucas Cranach, including a charming *Adam and Eve*. Perhaps the gallery's strongest suit is Flemish and Dutch art of the 15th–17th centuries. There are works by Geertgen tot Sint Jans, Jan Gossaert and the Brueghels, father and son. Pieter Brueghel the Elder's animated calendar painting, *The Haymaking*, has a rhythmic, almost dance-like quality. Outstanding among the later work is a portrait by Rembrandt, *Scholar in his Study* (1634), and several paintings by Rubens, including *Martyrdom of St Thomas* (1637–9), which was commissioned for the church in Malá Strana. By comparison, the Italian Renaissance is less well represented, although Andrea della Robbia, Sebastiano del Piombo and Pietro della Francesca all feature in the collection and there are some fine altar

✚	40B2
✉	Hradčanské náměstí 15, Praha 1
☎	2248 10758
🕐	Tue–Sun 10–6
🍴	Café (££)
Ⓜ	None
🚌	22, 23
🚊	None
♿	None
✋	Cheap
⟷	Pražský hrad (▶ 20–1), Vojenské muzeum (▶ 72)

panels by the 14th-century Sienese artist, Pietro Lorenzetti. Paintings by artists of the 18th-century Venetian school, including Tiepolo and Canaletto, and two fine Spanish works, El Greco's *Head of Christ* and a portrait by Goya of Don Miguel de Lardizabal, can also be found in the gallery. The superb collection of 19th- and 20th-century French art is now in the Veletrzny Palace (▶ 26).

Albrecht Dürer's Feast of the Rose Garlands

8
Strahovský Klášter
(Strahov Monastery)

The frescos in the Theological Hall were painted by Siard Nosecky, a canon of Strahov

Strahovní means 'watching over', and this ancient religious foundation, famous as a centre of learning, has been guarding the western approaches to Hradčany since the 12th century.

www.strahovskyklaster.cz

✚ 30A2

✉ Strahovské nádvoří, 1/132 Prahal, Hradčany

☎ 2205 166654

🕐 Daily 9–noon, 1–5

🍴 Restaurant (££)

🚇 None

🚌 22

🚋 None

♿ Good

✋ Moderate

↔ Loreta (▶ 19), Petřínské sady (▶ 64)

Above the baroque gateway is a statue of the founder of the Premonstratensian Order, St Norbert; to the left of the gate is the Church of St Roch, patron saint of plague victims, commissioned by Rudolf II in 1603 after Prague had narrowly escaped an epidemic. It is now used for modern art exhibitions. The twin-towered Abbey Church of the Nativity has a Romanesque core, but its present appearance dates from around 1750, when Anselmo Lurago remodelled the western façade. Mozart played the organ here on two occasions. The vaulted ceiling is sumptuously decorated with cartouches and frescos by Jiří Neunhertz, depicting the legend of St Norbert, whose remains were brought here from Magdeburg in 1627 and reburied in the chapel of St Ursula, on the left of the nave.

The library of the Strahov Monastery is more than 800 years old and among the finest in Europe. The Theological Hall, built in 1671–9 by Giovanni Orsi, has walls lined with elaborately carved bookcases, stacked with precious volumes and manuscripts. The Philosophical Hall dates from 1782–4, and its entire ceiling is covered with a delightful composition entitled *The Spiritual Development of Mankind*, by Franz Maulbertsch. The library contains over 130,000 volumes, including 2,500 books published before 1500, and 3,000 manuscripts. The oldest book, the 9th-century *Strahov Gospels*, is on show in the entrance.

9
Václavské náměstí
(Wenceslas Square)

Wenceslas Square really comes alive after dark, when its restaurants, cinemas and nightclubs attract a boisterous crowd.

Prague's most famous thoroughfare is actually an impressive 750m-long boulevard, dominated at the northern end by Josef Schulz's neo-Renaissance National Museum (►59). Once staging a horse market, Wenceslas Square was later a focus for political demonstration. When the Soviet army occupied Prague in August 1968 it was here that the distraught population gathered to protest. Several months later a student, Jan Palach, burned himself to death on the steps of the National Museum. Following the collapse of the Communist regime in December 1989, Václav Havel and Alexander Dubček appeared on the balcony of No 36 to greet their ecstatic supporters. Palach and other victims of the regime are commemorated in a small shrine in front of Josef Myslbek's equestrian statue of St Wenceslas, which was unveiled in 1912.

Wenceslas Square became a show-case for modern Czech architecture when the traditional two- and three-storey baroque houses were demolished in the 19th century. The neo-Renaissance Wiehl House was completed in 1896 and is decorated with florid sgraffito and statuary by Mikuláš Aleš. Many of the sumptuous art nouveau interiors and fittings in the Europa Hotel (No 25) have survived and are also worth investigating. The functionalist Koruna palác (No 1), a covered shopping arcade with a stunning glass dome dating from 1911, became the model for other passageways linking the square with the neighbouring streets (the Lucerna, at No 61, was built by Václav Havel's grandfather). The former insurance offices on the corner of Jindřišská could well have been the stuff of nightmares for Franz Kafka when he worked here as a clerk in 1906–7.

31C2

Václavské náměstí, Praha 1

Cafés (£), restaurants (££–£££)

Můstek, Muzeum

3, 9, 14, 24

None   Few

Free

Na Příkopě (►58), Národní muzeum (►59)

An equestrian statue of St Wenceslas presides over the square that bears his name

10
Veletržní Palác
(Veletrzny Palace)

31D3

Dukelskych hrdinů 47,
Praha 7

2243 01175

Tue–Sun 10–6

Restaurant (££); internet café (£)

Vltavská

5, 12, 17

Holešovice

Good

Moderate

Lapidárium (▶ 51)

The gallery's outstanding collection of modern Czech and European art is housed in a 1920s constructivist palace.

Designed by Oldřich Tyl and Josef Fuchs for the Prague Trade Fair of 1928, the enormous glass-fronted building was described by the famous modernist architect, Le Corbusier, as 'breathtaking'. The priceless French collection runs the gamut of Impressionist and Post-Impressionist artists. Among the highlights are *Two Women among the Flowers* (1875), by Monet, *Green Rye*, by Van Gogh (1889), and one of Gauguin's Tahiti paintings, *Flight* (1902). Picasso is represented by several contrasting paintings, ranging from an arresting, primitivist *Self Portrait*, dating from 1907, to *Clarinet* (1911), a classic example of analytic Cubism. There are also works by Braque, Chagall, Derain, Vlaminck, Raoul Dufy, Fernand Léger, Albert Marquet and Marie Laurencin. Among the sculptures are works by Rodin, Henri Laurens, and an unusual study of a dancer by Dégas.

Two Women among the Flowers *(1875) by Monet*, part of the gallery's outstanding French collection

French painting was a major source of inspiration for Czech artists seeking an alternative to the predominant German culture of the late 19th century. Jan Zrzavy, Bohumil Kubišta and Emil Filla all progressed from neo-Impressionism to more abstract styles. Kubišta's *Still Life with Funnel* (1910) was directly influenced by a similar study by Picasso. Other artists producing Cubist works at the time include Filla, Václav Špála and the sculptor Otto Gutfreund. The Czechs' affinity with French art becomes even more noticeable in the inter-war period, when the two countries were closely bound together by political and diplomatic ties. The crowning moment came in 1935, when the founder of the Surrealist movement, André Breton, visited Czechoslovakia at the invitation of the Prague Surrealists, Jindřich Štyrský, Vincenc Makovsky and Toyen (Marie Čermínová). The exhibition concludes with sections on post-war and contemporary art.

What
To See

Above: *mosaic on an upper facade in Staroměstské náměstí*
Right: *warrior in medieval costume at Mělník*

Prague

The view from the Charles Bridge at dusk: in the foreground, a procession of dramatic sculptures recedes into the distance; assembled behind them an extraordinary composition of gilded crosses, tented Gothic towers and baroque domes is silhouetted against the sunset. This is Prague in a nutshell. The city's extraordinary charms lie in the painstaking detail of its architecture – a gabled roof, an ornate railing, a sculpted house sign, a pair of Atlantes supporting a portal, a votive statue ensconced in a niche, a street lamp decorated with dancing maidens. Wherever one turns there is some magic to catch the eye.

> *' Prague always had two faces. She was officially German and unofficially Czech. Or she was officially Czech, but unofficially she had within herself a German city… She was officially Austrian and unofficially anti-Austrian. She was officially Catholic and unofficially anti-Christian. '*

WILLY LORENZ
To Bohemia with Love

Prague

Prague is best enjoyed at a leisurely pace. It's a compact city: the main sights are easily accessible on foot, and much of the central area is traffic free, with cafés and pubs on almost every street corner.

For sightseeing purposes, Prague falls naturally into its four medieval divisions: Hradčany (the area around the castle), Malá Strana (Lesser Quarter), Staré Město (Old Town) and Nové Město (New Town).

Hradčany is dominated by Prague Castle, primarily a tourist attraction with its cathedral, museums and galleries, but also a seat of government – the President and his ministers have their offices here.

Malá Strana, on the slopes beneath the castle, is distinguished by the green of its gardens and orchards, created in the 17th century by the aristocrats who built their palaces here. Crowning Malostranské náměstí is the majestic, green-domed Church of St Nicholas. Nearer the Vltava, the secluded neighbourhood of Na Kampě is perfect for a romantic evening stroll.

View towards Kostel Panny Marie před Týnem (Týn Church), one of many superb vistas to be enjoyed from the tower of Staroměstká radnice (Old Town Hall)

Beyond the Charles Bridge is Staré Město, historically the most important of the four towns. It grew up around Staroměstské náměstí, still a popular meeting place and one of the prettiest squares in Europe. The maze of narrow streets and arcaded courtyards conceals gabled houses, brightly painted shop fronts, churches and taverns.

The New Town – actually founded in the 14th century – is the commercial and administrative heart of the city. Even first-time visitors will probably have heard of Wenceslas Square (Václavské náměstí). 'Square' is actually a misnomer – it's really a long boulevard, lined with shops, hotels and nightclubs, that really comes alive after dark.

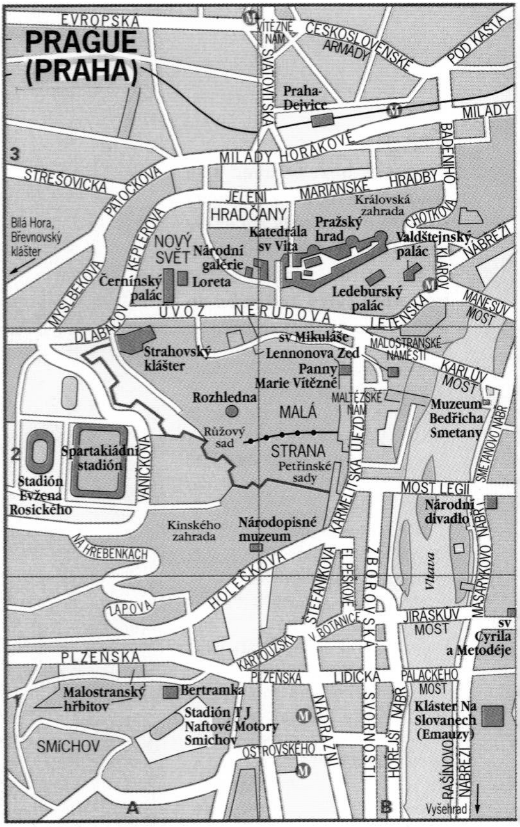

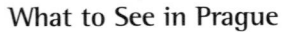

PRAGUE (PRAHA)

(Map showing central Prague with labelled locations including:)

EVROPSKA · VÍTĚZNÉ NÁM. · ČESKOSLOVENSKÉ ARMÁDY · POD KAŠTA · SVATOVITSKA · Praha-Dejvice · MILADY · BADENIHO · MILADY HORAKOVÉ · STRESOVICKA · PTLOCKOVA · MARIANSKE · HRADBY · JELENÍ · Královská zahrada · CHOTKOVA · KEPLEROVA · HRADČANY · Katedrála sv Víta · Pražský hrad · Bílá Hora, Břevnovský klášter · NOVÝ SVĚT · Národní galérie · Valdštejnský palác · NÁBŘEŽÍ · MYSLBEKOVA · Černínský palác · Loreta · Ledeburský palác · MANESŮV MOST · DLABAČOV · ÚVOZ · NERUDOVA · LETENSKA · sv Mikuláše · MALOSTRANSKÉ NÁMĚSTÍ · Strahovský klášter · Lennonova Zeď · Panny Marie Vítězné · KARLŮV MOST · Rozhledna · MALTEZSKE NAM. · Muzeum Bedřicha Smetany · Růžový sad · MALÁ STRANA · Spartakiádní stadión · Petřínské sady · SME TANOVO NABR · MOST LEGIÍ · Stadión Evžena Rosického · VANICKOVA · Národní divadlo · NA TREBENKACH · Kinského zahrada · Národopisné muzeum · Vltava · HOLECKOVA · LAPOVA · ZBOROVSKA · STEFANIKOVA · V BOTANICE · MASARYKOVO NABR · JIRÁSKŮV MOST · sv Cyrila a Metoděje · PLZEŇSKÁ · KARTOUZSKA · PLZEŇSKA · LIDICKA · PALACKÉHO MOST · Malostranský hřbitov · Bertramka · SVORNOSTI · Klášter Na Slovanech (Emauzy) · Stadión TJ Naftové Motory Smíchov · NA DRAZ KI · HORE JSI · RAŠÍNOVO NABREZI · SMÍCHOV · OSTROVSKÉHO · Vyšehrad

A · **B**

(Map grid reference: 3, 2)

What to See in Prague

ANEŽSKÝ KLÁŠTER (ST AGNES CONVENT)

😊😊😊

One of Prague's loveliest religious buildings, the convent was founded in 1234 by Agnes, sister of King Wenceslas I. St Agnes introduced the Order of Poor Clares into Bohemia and was the first abbess. Completed by the end of the 14th century and sacked by the Hussites in the 15th, the convent was eventually dissolved in 1782. An ambitious restoration programme of work was completed in the 1990s. The most impressive building is the Church of the Holy Saviour, an outstanding example of early Gothic architecture. Look out for the capitals, which are highly decorated with reliefs showing rulers of the Přemyslid dynasty. During the restoration the burial place of some of these kings and queens was unearthed,

---

Sidebar (left margin):

- 31C3
- U Milosrdných 17, Praha 1
- 2248 10758
- Tue–Sun 10–6
- Restaurant (££)
- Staroměstská, Náměstí Republiky
- 5, 17, 14, 26
- Good
- Moderate
- Josefov (▶ 17)

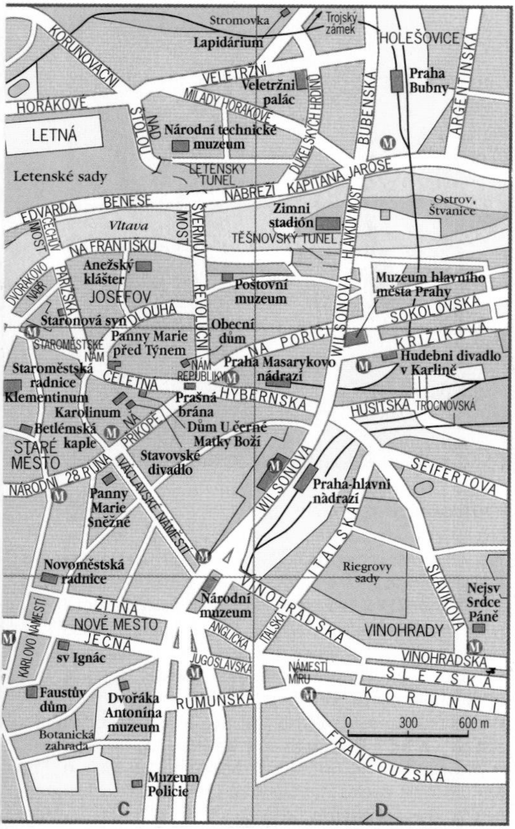

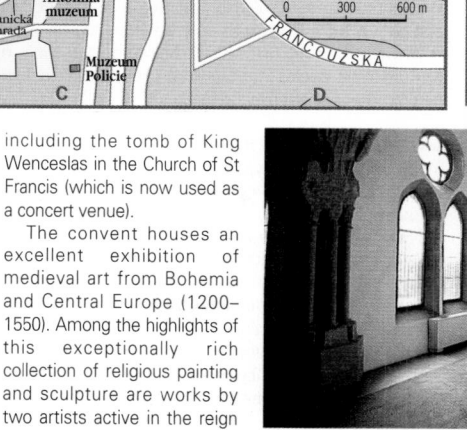

The timeless cloisters of Anežský klášter. The Gothic vaulting dates from the 14th century

including the tomb of King Wenceslas in the Church of St Francis (which is now used as a concert venue).

The convent houses an excellent exhibition of medieval art from Bohemia and Central Europe (1200–1550). Among the highlights of this exceptionally rich collection of religious painting and sculpture are works by two artists active in the reign of Charles IV: the Master of the Vyšší Brod Altar and Master Theodoric, whose lustrous portraits of the saints were intended for the chapel of Karlštejn Castle.

*18th-century style in the
Mozart Museum*

BERTRAMKA (MOZART MUSEUM)   ★★★

This hillside villa, the home of the soprano, Josefina
Dušek, and her composer husband František, was where
Wolfgang Amadeus Mozart stayed on his visits to Prague
in 1787 and 1791. Although the house was badly damaged
by fire in 1873, the rooms Mozart occupied have survived
and now contain a small exhibition on the composer and
his happy relationship with the Bohemian capital. The most
highly valued items, apart from the manuscripts, are his
harpsichord and a lock of his hair. But his presence can
best be felt in the lovely garden. It was here, on the night
of 28 October 1787, that Mozart dashed off the sublime
overture to his opera, *Don Giovanni*, just one night before
the première was given in the Estates Theatre (➤ 70).

BETLÉMSKÁ KAPLE (BETHLEHEM CHAPEL)   ★

The Bethlehem Chapel was built by followers of the radical
preacher Jan Milíč of Kroměříž in 1391–4. In 1402 a
lecturer at the university, Jan Hus, was appointed Rector
and drew huge crowds to his sermons, which were given
in Czech, rather than Latin. Hus was a charismatic figure,
but his attacks on the wealth and corruption of the Catholic
hierarchy did not endear him to his religious superiors. He
eventually overstepped the bounds of orthodoxy, arguing
that the Pope had no authority over the Bohemian Church
and that doctrine should be based on the scriptures alone.
Hus was excommunicated in 1412 and the Bethlehem
Chapel was closed. Summoned to defend his teachings at
the Council of Constance two years later, Hus consented
to leave the safe territory of Prague only after being issued
with a guarantee of safe conduct by the Emperor
Sigismund. But the Emperor went back on his word: Hus

was arrested, condemned as a heretic and, on 6 July 1415, burnt at the stake.

The decision to reconstruct the Chapel was taken in 1949. The prayer hall is trapezoid in form, the timber roof resting on plain stone supports. The total area measures 798sq m – ample space for the congregations of 3,000 who came to hear Hus speak. Painted on the walls are scenes from the life of the reformer and his followers, based on contemporary sources and painted by members of the Czech Academy of Fine Arts. Upstairs in the former preacher's house is an exhibition: 'The Bethlehem Chapel in Czech history and the tradition of non-Catholic thinking'.

A mural of the Annunciation painted on a gable in Betlémské náměstí (Bethelem Square): art bestows individuality on many of the buildings in Prague

BÍLÁ HORA (WHITE MOUNTAIN) ✪
In the space of an hour, on 8 November 1620, the Catholic Hapsburg army, under Maximilian of Bavaria, routed the Czech Protestants on this hillock outside Prague, deciding the fate of Bohemia for the next 300 years. The battle is commemorated by a small stone monument and the Church of Our Lady of Victories (1704–14).

Also in the park is the unusual Renaissance hunting lodge Letohrádek Hvĕdza (Star Castle), built in 1555–7. The six-pointed plan was the notion of its original owner, Ferdinand of Tyrol, son of the Governor of Bohemia. The castle now contains exhibitions devoted to the work of the writer Alois Jirásek and the painter, Mikoláš Aleš.

➕ Off map 30A3
✉ Vypich
☎ Castle: 2353 57938
🕐 Castle: May–Sep Tue–Sun 10–6, Oct–Apr Tue–Sun 10–5
🚋 8, 22
🚫 None
🎫 Castle: cheap
↔ Břevnovský klášter (► 34)

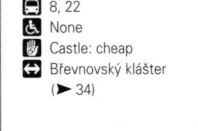

The stunning ceiling frescos in Břevnovský klášter have only recently been restored. They date from the 18th century

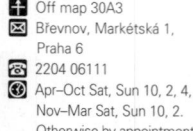

www.brevnov.cz
- 🚫 Off map 30A3
- ✉️ Břevnov, Markétská 1, Praha 6
- ☎️ 2204 06111
- 🕐 Apr–Oct Sat, Sun 10, 2, 4, Nov–Mar Sat, Sun 10, 2. Otherwise by appointment
- 🚋 22, 25
- 🚫 None
- 💰 Moderate
- ↔️ Bílá Hora (➤ 33)
- ❓ Guided tour only

- 🚫 31C2
- ✉️ Celetná, Praha 1
- 🍴 Cafés (££), restaurants (£££)
- 🚇 Náměstí Republiky
- 🚫 Few
- 💰 Free
- ↔️ Dům U Černé Matky Boží (➤ 38), Prašná brána (➤ 66), Staroměstská náměstí (➤ 68)

BŘEVNOVSKÝ KLÁŠTER (BŘEVNOV MONASTERY) ✪✪

There has been a monastery in Břevnov since AD 993 although the present baroque complex, designed by Christoph and Karl Dientzenhofer, dates from 1708–45. Recently the monastery was returned to the Benedictines and the restored buildings are being opened to the public. The remarkable St Margaret's Church, built over a Romanesque crypt, has breathtaking oval ceiling frescos by Johann Steinfels depicting scenes from the legend of St Adalbert, while the Theresian Hall has a magnificent painting of Blessed Günther by Kosmas Assam.

CELETNÁ ✪

The street of bakers is one of the oldest in the city and was on the royal processional route. Its handsomely decorated baroque façades conceal in many cases Romanesque or Gothic foundations. An exception is the Cubist House of the Black Madonna (➤ 38). The house at No 36, with the wrought-iron balcony supported by Atlantes, is the former mint. Some of Prague's best known restaurants are on Celetná: House At the Golden Vulture (No 22), At the Spider (No 17) and At the Golden Stag (No 11). Celetná is also a good place to shop for glassware, jewellery and antiques.

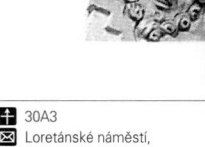

ČERNÍNSKÝ PALÁC (ČERNÍN PALACE) ✪

So much stone was used in the construction of this vast palace, with a façade stretching the entire length of Loretánské náměstí (135m), that it was said that the builders were being paid by the cubic metre. Certainly the palace's original owner, Count Jan Černín of Chudenice, Imperial Ambassador to Venice, spared no expense on the interior decoration – the work of the sculptor, Matyás Braun and the painter, Vaclav Reiner, among others. In 1948, 20 years after the palace was acquired by the Ministry of Foreign Affairs, Jan Masaryk, son of the founder of Czechoslovakia and the only non-Communist member of the government, fell to his death from an upper floor window into the courtyard below. It is now widely believed that Masaryk was murdered on the orders of Stalin.

- ✚ 30A3
- ✉ Loretánské náměstí, Praha 1
- ☎ 2241 81111
- ⏰ Not open to public
- 🚌 22
- ♿ None
- ↔ Loreta (► 19), Strahovský klášter (► 24)

The stupendous façade of the 17th-century Černínský palác dominates the western end of Hradčany

CHRÁM PANNY MARIE SNĚŽNÉ (OUR LADY OF THE SNOWS) ✪

Founded in 1347 by Charles IV, Our Lady of the Snows was to have been the largest church in Prague – 40m high and 110m long – but the outbreak of the Hussite wars interrupted work on the building. In 1603 the completed choir was restored to the Franciscans and given a baroque facelift as well as a new vaulted ceiling. Otherwise, all that remains of the 14th-century church are the crumbling pediment over the north gateway and the pewter font. The Franciscan Gardens near the south wall were originally part of the monastery grounds and are now a public park.

CHRÁM SVATÉHO MIKULÁŠ (► 16 TOP TEN)

- ✚ 31C2
- ✉ Jungmannovo náměstí 18, Praha 1
- ☎ 2244 90350
- ⏰ Daily 9–6 (except during mass). Also open for concerts – tickets available at the door
- 🚇 Můstek
- ♿ Few
- 💵 Free
- ↔ Václavské náměstí (► 25)

35

Food & Drink

You can be sure of one thing when you eat out in Prague – or anywhere else in the Czech Republic, for that matter: you will not go hungry. All the national dishes are incredibly rich and filling, and portions are gargantuan.

Meat and Veg

Pork is still a staple of the traditional Czech meal

Czech cuisine is heavily meat-based. Pork, beef and chicken are all standard fare – but the pig is king. Popular dishes include pork with dumplings and *sauerkraut* (pickled cabbage), roast duck with bacon dumplings, and roast beef with a sour cream sauce. *Wiener schnitzel*, known to the Czechs as *smažený řízek*, is another favourite. In expensive restaurants, you're likely to encounter game – venison, pheasant, hare or even wild boar. Most meat is boiled or roasted and served swimming in gravy and accompanied by potatoes or dumplings (*knedlíky*).

Fresh vegetables, other than the ubiquitous *sauerkraut*, are appearing on menus with increasing frequency and you'll usually be able to order a side salad of tomato and onions, cucumber or just plain lettuce. Some restaurants even serve noodles or pasta as an accompaniment to standard Czech items. But vegetarians should note that

many apparently meatless dishes are cooked in animal fat. The best advice is to declare yourself at the outset: *Jsem vegetarian (-ka* for the feminine form).

Of the fish dishes, boiled carp served in melted butter, roasted pike, fillet of trout cooked in a green pepper sauce and smoked salmon are all delicious. Try to leave some room for dessert, but don't count the calories. Pancakes may be filled with ice cream, jam or stewed fruit. Apple strudel and plum dumplings are reliable stand-bys.

Beer

Czech beer is justifiably famous and is fully appreciated by the Czechs themselves – the Republic boasts the highest *per capita* consumption in the world: 153.6 litres annually. Plzeň produces the clear golden nectar known as Pilsner Urquell in Germany and locally as Plzeňský Prazdroj. Gambrinus is another common brand. The other main centre of beer production is the southern Bohemian town of České Budějovice, Budweis in German. Don't be misled by the name – the American beer, Budweiser, and the Czech brew, Budvar, have nothing in common. All these brews are delicious, but local Prague beers like Staropramen and Braník are just as good. If you fancy trying a dark (*tmave*) beer, head for the famous pub known as U Fleků, which produces its own brand. The generic term for beer is *pivo*.

Wines and Spirits

Most Czech wine is produced in the warmer, more sheltered parts of southern Moravia and is consumed locally, rather than exported. The best of the red wines is Frankovka or Vavřinecké – Tramín is a reliable white variety. The Mělník region, just north of Prague, produces a small amount of wine of variable quality (sometimes none at all, if the weather is bad). A dry white wine known as Rulandské bílé is probably the best, and can often be found on menus. There are three types of liqueur worth sampling: Borovicka, a fiery, juniper-flavoured spirit with the impact of an Italian grappa, which should be treated with the same respect; Slivovice, a plum brandy and, best of all, the wonderfully aromatic Becherovka, a herb-based drink concocted in the spa town of Karlovy Vary.

Czech beer is renowned throughout the world. Pilsner lager was first brewed in Plzeň in 1842

31C2
Řetězová 222/3, Praha 1
May–Sep Tue–Sun 10–6;
currently closed for
restoration
Národní třída
6, 9, 18, 22
Moderate
Betlémská kaple (➤ 32),
Karlův most (➤ 40),
Klementinum (➤ 44)

31C2
Celetná 34, Praha 1
2242 11746
Tue–Sun 10–6. Closed 1
Jan, Easter Mon, 1 and 8
May, 5 and 6 July, 28
Oct, 24–6 Dec
Cafés (££), restaurants
(£££)
Náměstí Republiky
None
Moderate
Celetná (➤ 34), Prašná
brána (➤ 66)

*The famous statue of the
Black Madonna that gives
the house on Celetná its
name*

31C2
Staroměstská náměstí 13,
Praha 1
2248 27526
Tue–Sun 10–6. Closed 1
Jan, Easter Mon, 1, 8
May, 5, 6 July, 28 Oct,
24–6 Dec
Staroměstská
Cheap
Celetná (➤ 34), Kostel
Panny Marie před Týnem
(➤ 46), Kostel Svatého
Mikuláše (➤ 48)

38

DŮM PÁNŮ Z KUNŠTÁTU A PODĚBRAD ✪✪
(HOUSE OF THE LORDS KUNSTAT AND PODEBRAD)

The medieval chambers of this former palace, with original Romanesque cross-vaulted ceilings and fireplaces, are now open to the public. Dating from about 1200, they once formed the ground floor of a building which was enlarged in the 15th century for the Lords of Kunstat and Poděbrady. There is a small exhibition on its most famous resident, George of Podebrad, who became King of Bohemia in 1457.

DŮM U ČERNÉ MATKY BOŽÍ ✪✪
(HOUSE OF THE BLACK MADONNA)

While Cubist painting is common in Europe, Cubist architecture is unique to Bohemia. Designed by Josef Gočár in 1911–12, this innovative building was right at the cutting edge of the modernist movement, with its façades broken into multiple planes in order to create an unusual interplay of light and shade. Behind a grille on the first floor is the statue of the Black Mother of God, which gives the building its name.

Inside is a permanent exhibition on Czech Cubism 1911–19.

DŮM U KAMENNÉHO ZVONU ✪✪
(HOUSE AT THE STONE BELL)

This magnificent Gothic tower with its characteristic hipped roof was built as a palace for King John of Luxembourg around 1340. The sculpted decoration of the west façade was rediscovered in the 1960s, having long been concealed by a rococo facelift. Make sure you don't overlook the stone bell on the corner of the building which gives the house its name. Concerts and exhibitions are held here and visitors can see original Gothic features, including extensive fragments of medieval wall painting. The ceiling beams, delicately painted with floral motifs, date from the reign of Charles IV.

DVOŘÁKA ANTONÍNA MUZEUM (DVORAK MUSEUM) ✪

This beautiful baroque mansion, built by Kilian Dientzenhofer in 1717–20 for a prominant Czech nobleman, acquired its present name, Villa Amerika, in the 19th century – there was an eating house of that name near by. It is therefore entirely appropriate that the building now honours the composer of the 'New World' symphony, Antonín Dvořák (1841–1904).

Unfortunately, the palatial interior, with partly restored frescos by Johann Schlor, is not really suitable for such an intimate exhibition, especially given the composer's decidedly modest background and lifestyle. (His apartment on Žitná Street, not far from here, was demolished long ago.) The exhibits, spread over two floors, include autographed scores, photographs, busts and portraits, correspondence with fellow musicians (the composers, Brahms and Tchaikovsky, and the German conductor, Hans von Bulöw, were among Dvořák's friends and admirers) and a number of personal effects including his viola, Bible and spectacles. The first floor is also used for concerts.

www.nm.cz
✚ 31C1
✉ Ke Karlovu 20, Praha 2
☎ 2249 18013
🕐 Tue–Sun 10–5
Ⓜ IP Pavlova
🚌 272 ♿ Few
💵 Cheap
↔ Muzeum Policie (► 56)

Above: *the Czech composer Antonín Dvořák's piano, one of the exhibits on display in the Villa Amerika*

EXPOZICE FRANZE KAFKY (FRANZ KAFKA EXHIBITION) ✪

A sculpted relief marks the site of the house where Franz Kafka was born in 1883. Only the doorway of the original building, 'At the Tower', remains following a fire in 1887. There is a photographic exhibition of Kafka's life on the ground floor.

Left: *this arresting sculpture by Karel Hladík marks the site of Franz Kafka's birthplace*

✚ 31C2
✉ Náměstí Franze Kafky 3, Praha 1
☎ None
🕐 Tue–Fri 10–6, Sat 10–5
🍴 Café (£), restaurants (££–£££) near by
Ⓜ Staroměstská
💵 Cheap
↔ Celetná (► 34), Dům U Kamenného Zvonu (► 38), Kostel Panny Marie před Týnem (► 46), Kostel Svatého Mikuláše (► 48), Muzeum Českého Skla (► 55), Staroměstská náměstí (► 68)

Did you know ?

'Prague does not let go...This little mother has claws', Franz Kafka once confided to his diary. His love-hate relationship with the city is reflected in the novels The Trial *and* The Castle, *where Prague's menacing presence looms over the characters.*

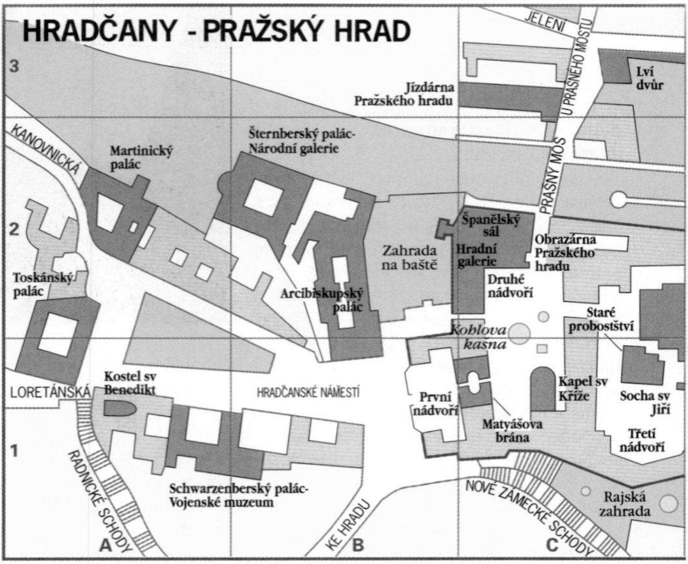
HRADČANY - PRAŽSKÝ HRAD
3
2
1
A
B
C
Jízdárna Pražského hradu
Lví dvůr
JELENÍ
U PRAŠNÉHO MOSTU
KANOVNICKÁ
Martinický palác
Šternberský palác-Národní galerie
PRAŠNÝ MOST
Španělský sál
Hradní galerie
Obrazárna Pražského hradu
Zahrada na baště
Druhé nádvoří
Toskánský palác
Arcibiskupský palác
Staré proboštství
Kohlova kasna
Kostel sv Benedikt
LORETÁNSKÁ
HRADČANSKÉ NÁMĚSTÍ
První nádvoří
Kapel sv Kříže
Socha sv Jiří
Matyášova brána
Třetí nádvoří
RADNICKÉ SCHODY
Schwarzenberský palác-Vojenské muzeum
KE HRADU
NOVÉ ZÁMECKÉ SCHODY
Rajská zahrada

- 40B1
- Hradcanské náměstí, Praha 1
- Café (£)
- 22
- Few
- Pražský hrad (➤ 20–1)

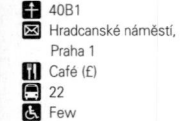

Right: *street musicians entertaining the tourists in Hradčany*

- 30B2
- Karlův most, Praha 1
- Lesser Town Tower: Apr–Oct daily 10–6. Old Town Tower: Apr, May, Oct 10–7, Jun–Sep 10–10, Mar 10–6, Nov–Feb 10–5
- Staroměstská 12, 22
- Good Towers: cheap

HRADČANSKÉ NÁMĚSTÍ (HRADČANY SQUARE) ✪

This is a square of stunning Renaissance and baroque façades. The Archbishop's Palace (No 16) was given its eye-catching rococo facelift in 1764 by the architect Johan Wirch, and is adorned with the family crest of the original owner, Archbishop Antonín Příchovský. Across the square is the Renaissance Schwarzenberg Palace. The yellow-fronted Tuscany Palace (No 5), once owned by the Duke of Tuscany (whose coat of arms is emblazoned above the portal) dates from 1689–91. Jaroslav Bořita of Martinitz, one of the defenestrated ministers of 1618, gave his name to the handsome palace at No 8 with its figurative sgraffito illustrating the story of Joseph and Potiphar and other biblical tales.

JOSEFOV (➤ 17 TOP TEN)

KARLŮV MOST (CHARLES BRIDGE) ✪✪✪

This remarkable sandstone bridge, designed in 1357 by Petr Parléř for King Charles IV, links the Old Town with the Lesser Quarter. In 1657 a bronze crucifix with a Hebrew inscription was erected on the bridge – the only ornament at that time. The idea caught on and now more than 30 sculptures adorn the parapets. Perhaps the finest of them, by Matthias Braun (1710), shows St Luitgard kissing Christ's wounds in a vision. The figure with the starry halo is St John of Nepomuk whose tortured body was hurled

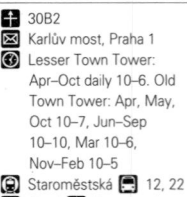

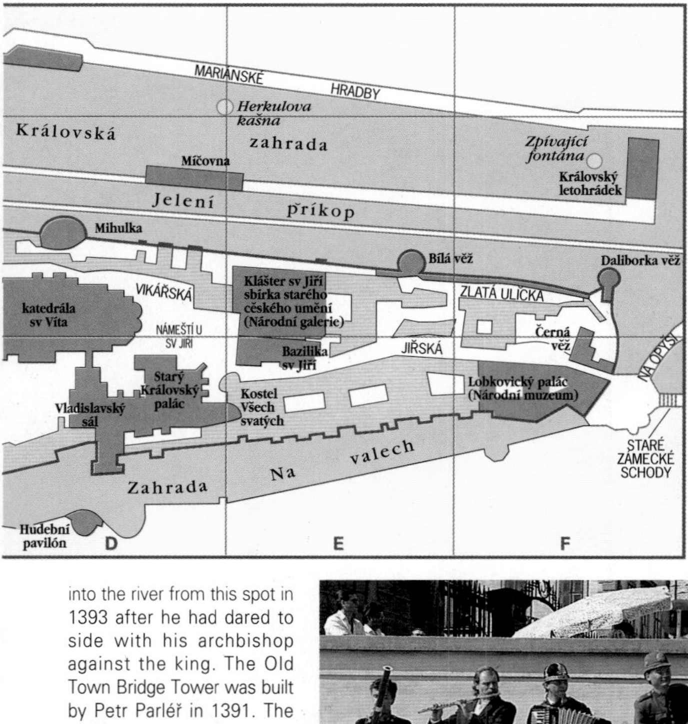

Map

MARIÁNSKÉ HRADBY

Královská

Herkulova kašna

zahrada

Zpívající fontána

Míčovna

Královský letohrádek

Jelení příkop

Mihulka

VIKÁŘSKÁ

Bílá věž

Daliborka věž

katedrála sv Víta

NÁMĚŠTÍ U SV JIŘÍ

Klášter sv Jiří sbírka starého českého umění (Národní galerie)

ZLATÁ ULIČKA

Bazilika sv Jiří

JIŘSKÁ

Černá věž

NA OPYŠI

Starý Královský palác

Kostel Všech svatých

Lobkovický palác (Národní muzeum)

Vladislavský sál

Zahrada

Na valech

STARÉ ZÁMECKÉ SCHODY

Hudební pavilón

D

E

F

into the river from this spot in 1393 after he had dared to side with his archbishop against the king. The Old Town Bridge Tower was built by Petr Parléř in 1391. The sculptures above the arch show St Vitus in the company of Kings Wenceslas IV and Charles IV – the views from the gallery are spectacular. Today the Charles Bridge is made all the more colourful by the buskers and street traders

who have made it their own in recent years.

KAROLINUM ✪

Founded in 1348 by Charles IV, the Karolinum is the oldest university in Central Europe. It acquired the house of the former mint master, Johlin Rothlev of Kutna Hora, in 1383 (until then classes had been held in churches or private houses). Although Rothlev's house was completely remod-elled in the 18th century by František Kaňka, the exquisite oriel window protruding from the façade on Ovocny trh is a reminder of its medieval origins. The Karolinum has long outgrown its original premises, which are currently occupied by the university Rectorate.

🚩 31C2
✉ Železná 9, Praha 1
☎ 2242 28600
Ⓜ Můstek
♿ None
🔄 Celetná (► 34), Staroměstská náměstí (► 68), Stavovské divadlo (► 70)

For nearly 700 years the Karlův most (Charles Bridge) has been the main link between Staré Město (the Old Town) and Mala Straná (the Lesser Quarter)

KATEDRÁLA SVATÉHO VÍTA (▶ 18 TOP TEN)

KLÁŠTER SVATÉHO JIŘÍ (ST GEORGE'S CONVENT AND BASILICA) ✪✪✪

St George's Convent houses the National Gallery's collection of Czech Mannerist and baroque art (see below), and adjoining it is the Basilica, one of the oldest religious foundations in Prague, dating back to 920 and reconstructed in its present Romanesque form after a fire in 1142 (the baroque façade is a 17th-century addition). To the right of the entrance to the crypt is the painted wooden tomb of the founder, Prince Vratislav. Climb the ornate stairway for a good view of the faded 13th-century frescos, depicting the Heavenly Jerusalem, in the apse, and of the equally striking Renaissance paintings in the Chapel of St Ludmilla. Also regular concerts in the Basilica.

- 🏛 41E2
- ✉ Jirské námsětí 33, Hradčany
- ☎ 2573 20889
- 🕐 Tue–Sun 10–6; basilica daily 9–4; gallery Tue–Sun 10–6
- 🍴 Café (£), restaurants (££–£££) near by
- 🚌 22 ♿ Few
- 💷 Moderate
- ↔ Pražský hrad (▶ 20–1),

The Romanesque Basilica dates from 1142

The exhibition in the convent begins with a small but valuable display of Mannerist works by artists from the court of the Emperor Rudolph II: Bartholomeus Spranger, Hans von Aschen, Adrian de Vries – don't miss his superb sculpture *Stepping Horse* (c1610) and Benedikt Wurzelbauer. The National Gallery's outstanding collection of baroque paintings and sculptures can be found on the first floor. Many of the Bohemian and Silesian artists exhibited here played a key role in beautifying Prague's churches and monasteries in the 17th and 18th centuries. They include Škreta, impressively represented by altarpieces, portraits and easel paintings, Petr Brandl, Václav Reiner and the sculptor, Matyáš Braun. Look out for some outstanding portraits by Jan Kupecky, notably *Self-Portrait with Wife* (after 1725) and Ignác Platzer, a master of the rococo whose commissions included the decoration of the Church of St Nicholas in the Lesser Town.

+ 31C3
✉ U Starého hřbitova 3a,
    Praha 1
☎ 2248 19456
🕐 Apr–Oct Sun–Fri 9–6,
    Nov–Mar Sun–Fri 9–4:30.
    Closed Jewish hols
🚇 Staroměstská
🚊 17, 18
♿ Few
💰 Moderate
↔ Obřadní síň (➤ 64), Stary
    židovský hřbitov (➤ 69)

KLAUSOVÁ SYNAGÓGA (KLAUSEN SYNAGOGUE) ✪

A number of religious schools and other buildings known as *klausen* were cleared away after the great fire of 1689 to make way for this early baroque synagogue. The fine interior, with barrel-vaulted roof, stuccoed ceiling ornamentation and stained-glass windows, has been restored and now contains an exhibition on local Jewish customs and traditions, including old Hebrew manuscripts and prints, beautifully worked Torah ornaments, skull caps embroidered in satin and velvet, bronze Hanukkah lamps and a curious wooden alms box (*c*1800) with a supplicating hand and arm. The marble Holy Ark, made in 1696 at the expense of Samuel Openheim, has also been restored.

+ 31C2
✉ Mariánské náměstí 5,
    Praha 1
☎ 6032 31241
🕐 Tours on hour Mon–Fri
    2–6, Sat, Sun, hols 11–6
    (buy ticket in advance)
🚇 Staroměstská
🚊 17, 18   ♿ Few
↔ Karlův most (➤ 40),
    Křižovnické náměstí
    (➤ 50)

*The magnificent Baroque
Hall of the Klementinum
is now part of the
National Library*

KLEMENTINUM ✪

When the Emperor Ferdinand I invited the Jesuits to Prague in 1556 to spearhead the Counter-Reformation, they moved into the former monastery of St Clement. In the 17th century the Karolinum (➤ 41) merged with the Klementinum, giving them a monopoly of higher education, and they undertook a building programme which lasted over 150 years. The walls of the baroque fortress enclosed a college, schools, churches, a library, a theatre, an observatory and a printing shop. When the Jesuit Order was dissolved in 1773 the complex was taken over by the university; today it belongs to the National Library. The Klementinum is being renovated, but there are guided tours of the library and the astronomical tower with panoramic views across the city. The Chapel of Mirrors (1724–30) is also open for concerts.

A Walk Around Josefov

The area to the north of the Old Town, now known as Josefov, was first settled by Jews in the 13th century. Most of the surviving sights and monuments date from the 16th and 17th centuries.

Start in Maiselova, heading away from Old Town Square, and pass the Maisel Synagogue. At the crossroads, turn left onto Široká. On your right is the Pinkas Synagogue.

Distance
1km

Time
2hrs

Start/end point
Metro Staroměstská
✚ 31C2

Lunch
Franz Kafka (£)
✉ Široká 12
☎ 2223 18945

The Maisel Synagogue (➤ 53) has an exhibition of ceremonial silverware from Bohemia and Moravia. The Pinkas Synagogue (➤ 65) is now a memorial to Holocaust victims.

Leave by the back entrance of the Pinkas Synagogue, which leads into the Old Jewish Cemetery (➤ 69).

The oldest graves here date from the 15th century. At the opposite gate is the Ceremonial Hall and the Klausen Synagogue (➤ 44).

Walk east along Ust Hřbitova Červená to the junction with Maiselova.

The grave of the renowned rabbi Jehuda Löw in the Starý židovský hřbitov (Old Jewish Cemetery). Visitors place pebbles on the tomb as a mark of respect

On your right you will find the late baroque Town Hall, now the Jewish Community Centre, the High Synagogue and the 13th-century step-gabled Old-New Synagogue (➤ 69).

Continue along Ust Hřbitova Červená between the synagogues, then turn right onto Pařížská. Turn left at Široká and cross Dušní to Vnská.

Moorish-style motifs decorate the interior of the Spanish Synagogue (on the corner), which dates from 1867–8.

Golden statue of the Virgin between the towers of Kostel Panny Marie před Týnem

KOSTEL PANNY MARIE PŘED TÝNEM 😊😊
(CHURCH OF OUR LADY BEFORE TÝN)

Most impressive at night when its gaunt, black steeples are eerily lit, Our Lady before Týn is the Old Town parish church. Although building started in 1380 under the supervision of Petr Parléř, work on the towers was not completed until 1511. For most of that period Týn Church was the stronghold of the Hussite Utraquists, who insisted on taking communion in both kinds (the symbolic gilded

chalice which hung from the gable was melted down after the Counter-Reformation to make an effigy of the Virgin). The beautifully sculpted portal dates from 1390. The restored interior is an uneasy marriage of Gothic and baroque styles. Over the high altar are paintings by Karol Škréta, dating from 1640–60, while Gothic features include a *pietà*, a 15th-century pulpit and a pewter font (1414). In front of the high altar is the tomb of the Danish astronomer, Tycho Brahe (1546–1601).

KOSTEL SVATÉHO CYRILA A METODĚJE 😊
(CHURCH OF SS CYRIL AND METHODIUS)

A plaque on the bullet-scarred wall of this Orthodox cathedral commemorates the Free Czech paratroopers who died here on 18 June 1942, after taking part in the assassination of the Nazi Governor of Bohemia and Moravia, Reinhard Heydrich. Members of the Czech Orthodox community hid them in the crypt, but they were discovered, and committed suicide rather than fall into enemy hands. SS Cyril and Methodius designated a National Memorial to the victims of the Heydrich Terror.

KOSTEL PANNY MARIE VÍTĚZNÉ 😊
(OUR LADY VICTORIOUS)

The chief attraction of this 17th-century church is a wax effigy of the infant Jesus, usually known by its Italian name Il Bambino di Praga. Believed to have miracle-working properties, the statue was brought from Spain in 1628 by

The lofty baroque nave of Kostel Svatého Jakuba in Stare Město (the Old Town)

Polxena of Lobkowicz and presented to the Carmelite nuns, who continue to care for its 39 embroidered outfits.

KOSTEL SVATÉHO JAKUBA (ST JAMES'S CHURCH) ✪✪✪

The Minorite Order of Franciscans commissioned this baroque church in 1689 after its 13th-century predecessor had been destroyed in a fire. The paintings in the nave, galleries and 21 side altars are by a variety of artists, including Franz Voget, Petr Brandl and Václav Reiner, who also contributed the effulgent *Martyrdom of St James* over the high altar. Equally remarkable is the stunning tomb of the Chancellor of Bohemia, Count Vratislav of Mitrovice, on the left-hand side of the nave. It was sculpted in marble and sandstone by Ferdinand Brokof. A shrivelled arm which dangles just inside the door belonged to a jewel thief caught stealing here in the 16th century.

St James's is renowned for its musical tradition. A choir sings at high mass on Sundays, accompanied on the organ, a splendid baroque instrument dating from 1702. There are regular concerts and recitals here.

- ✚ 31C2
- ✉ Malá Stupartská 6, Praha 1
- 🕐 Mon–Sat 9:30–12:15, 2–4. Sun except for services 8, 9, 10:30, also for concerts
- Ⓜ Můstek
- ♿ None
- 💲 Free
- ↔ Celetná (➤ 34), Staroměstské náměstí (➤ 68)

47

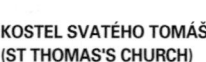

+ 31C2
✉ Staroměstské náměstí, Praha 1
🕐 Mon 12–4, Tue–Sat 10–4, Sun 10:30 (mass), 12–3, also for concerts
🍴 Cafés (£), restaurants (££–£££) near by
Ⓜ Staroměstská
♿ None 🎫 Free

KOSTEL SVATÉHO MIKULÁŠE (ST NICHOLAS'S CHURCH) ✪✪

This beautifully proportioned baroque masterpiece was designed by the prolific Kilian Dientzenhofer in 1732 and completed three years later. (The sculptures of saints are by Antonín Braun.) St Nicholas stands on the site of a much older Gothic church. When, in the spirit of the Enlightenment, the Emperor Joseph II evicted the Benedictines later in the 18th century, on the grounds that they were not performing a useful function, the church was used as a warehouse and fell into disrepair. It was saved during World War I when the commander of the occupying garrison invited local artists to restore Kosmas Asam's frescos of SS Nicholas and Benedict in the dome. In other respects the building lacks the exuberance of baroque ornamentation.

A baroque flourish on the door of Kostel Svatého Mikuláše

Since 1920 St Nicholas has belonged to the Czech Reformed (Hussite) Church and is regularly used for concerts.

+ 30B3
✉ Letenská, Praha 1
🕐 Daily and for services
🍴 Cafés (£), restaurants (££) near by
Ⓜ Malostranská
🚌 12, 22
♿ None
🎫 Free
🔗 Malostranské náměstí (► 53), Nerudova (► 60–1), Valdštejnský palác (► 71)

KOSTEL SVATÉHO TOMÁŠE (ST THOMAS'S CHURCH) ✪✪

The spire of this attractive church rises impressively above the rooftops of Lesser Town Square. Founded in 1285, at the same time as the neighbouring Augustinian monastery, it has undergone many reincarnations over the centuries, the latest in 1723–31 when Kilian Dientzenhofer completely remodelled the Gothic church after it had been damaged by lightning. The interior is captivating, with glorious ceiling frescos by Václav Reiner depicting the life of St Augustine and, in the dome, the legend of St Thomas. Amazingly, he completed the work in just two years. Other distinguished artists, including Karel Škréta and the sculptor, Ferdinand Brokoff, also contributed to the décor, while the paintings (copies) over the high altar, of St Thomas and St Augustine, were commissioned from Rubens (the originals are now in the Šternberský Palác, ► 23).

A Walk Along the Royal Route

This walk follows the processional route taken by the kings and queens of Bohemia at their coronation.

Start at Obecní Dům (► 61) and head down Celetná to Staroměstské náměstí.

The leading burghers and dignitaries of the town rode out to welcome their new monarch at the Powder Gate (► 66), before accompanying him past the cheering crowds on Celetná (► 34) to Old Town Square (► 68). Here the procession halted to hear professions of loyalty from the rector of the University and the mayor and council in the Town Hall (► 22).

Cross the square to Malé náměstí and on to Karlova. At the end of Karlova, cross Křižovnická to Křížovnícké náměstí (► 50) and the Charles Bridge (► 40).

Today Karlova is a quaint, twisting street, lined with galleries and souvenir shops, overshadowed by the fortress-like walls of the former Jesuit stronghold, the Klementinum (► 44). As the procession passed the Church of St Francis the King was greeted by the Order of the Knights of the Cross with the Red Star (► 50).

Cross the River Vltava to Mostecká and follow Malostranské náměstí round onto Nerudova (► 60). Climb the hill to the Castle.

At the Lesser Quarter Bridge Tower, the mayor handed over the keys to the city and the King then continued through Malostranské náměstí (► 53) to the tumultuous sound of bells from St Nicholas's Church (► 48). The processional route ends at the Matthias Gate, the ceremonial entrance to Prague Castle.

Distance
2½ km

Time
1½ hrs without stops

Start point
Obecní Dům
⊠ Náměstí Republiky
✚ 31C2

End point
Pražský hrad
✚ 30B3

Lunch
Caffé–Ristorante Italia (££)
⊠ Nerudova 17
☎ 2575 32818

Marionettes are among the more colourful souvenirs on sale in Staroměstské náměstí (Old Town Square)

Dramatic sunrise over Křižovnické náměstí

KRÁLOVSKÁ ZAHRADA (ROYAL GARDENS)

These delightful gardens with wonderful views were laid out in 1534 in the style of the Italian Renaissance. Four years later, work began on the Belvedere, the handsome summer house presented by Ferdinand I to his wife, Anna Jagiello. A magnificent arcaded building with a copper roof resembling an upturned ship's hull, it was completed in 1564 by Paolo Della Stella, who also designed the mytho-logical reliefs. The palace is now used for exhibitions. The sgraffitoed Ball Game Hall at the eastern end of the gardens is the work of the Czech architect, Bonifaz Wohlmut, and was given its name by courtiers who played a form of tennis here. Tulips grow in the gardens every spring – another reminder of Ferdinand I, who introduced the flower to Europe from Turkey in the 16th century. Near the entrance is the Lion's Court, once a menagerie exhibiting bears, panthers, tigers and other wild beasts.

KŘIŽOVNICKÉ NÁMĚSTÍ (KNIGHTS OF THE CROSS SQUARE) 🌟🌟

Dominating the eastern side of this square, which is named after the 13th-century guardians of the Judith Bridge, is the façade of the Klementinum and the Jesuit Church of St Saviour (➤ 44). The knights' own Church of St Francis, a baroque building which dates from 1679–88, is across the square. An exhibition at the side of the church includes a visit to the medieval crypt, which is decorated with garishly painted baroque stalactites. The treasury contains a collection of jewelled monstrances, chalices, reliquaries and other religious objects which belonged to the Order, some dating back to the 16th century. Perhaps of greatest interest is a surviving span of the 12th-century Judith Bridge, complete with water stairs.

Standing in front of the church, near today's Charles Bridge, is an imposing statue of Charles IV, designed in 1848 by Jan Bendl.

LAPIDÁRIUM ●●●

Located in an art nouveau pavilion in the Exhibition Ground, this is a fascinating review of Czech sculpture from the 11th to the 19th century, with explanatory leaflets in English and other languages. One of the earliest exhibits is a beautifully ornamented column from the crypt of the 11th-century Basilica of St Vitus; other displays include the Krocín fountain, a remarkable Renaissance monument which used to stand on Old Town Square, and the 9m-high Bear Gate, also known as the Slavata Portal, which once adorned a beautiful baroque garden in the Smíchov district. Ferdinand Brokoff's statues of St Ignatius and St Francis Xavier, now adorning the Charles Bridge, are copies. The originals exhibited here were torn down in the floods of 1890.

➕ 31D3
✉ Holešovice, Výstaviště 422, Praha 7
☎ 2333 75636
🕐 Tue–Fri 12–5, Sat–Sun 10–5
🍴 Cafés (£)
🚇 Nádraží Holešovice
🚊 5, 12, 17
♿ Few 👋 Cheap
↔ Veletržní Palác (▶ 26)

'Give peace a chance' is the sentiment expressed on Lennonova Zed'

LENNONOVA ZED' (LENNON WALL) ●

Hidden among the embassies and palaces of the Malá Strana, this stretch of wall became a thorn in the side of the Communist authorities following John Lennon's death in 1980, when it was painted with democratic and pacifist graffiti. A game of cat-and-mouse ensued between police and artists as the wall was continually whitewashed and repainted. After the Velvet Revolution it was allowed to remain, at the request of the French ambassador.

➕ 30B2
✉ Velkopřevorské náměstí
🚊 12, 27, 57
♿ Good
👋 None
↔ Karlův most (▶ 40), Maltézské náměstí (▶ 54)

LORETA (▶ 19 TOP TEN)

MAISELOVA SYNAGÓGA (MAISEL SYNAGOGUE) ✪✪

Originally a Renaissance temple, built in 1591 for Mayor Mordechai Maisel (➤ 17), financier to Emperor Rudolph II, the synagogue has a beautifully restored interior, which preserves some of the 16th-century stone carving.

The building is now used to house an exhibition of sacred religious objects, which include items associated with the focus of Jewish worship – the Torah. This consists of the five books of Moses, handwritten on rolls of parchment by scribes. By tradition the rollers would be elaborately decorated with finials, shields and crowns, superbly wrought in silver or brass and often gilded or encrusted with jewels. Examples of the richly embroidered mantles in which the Torah was wrapped are also on display in the synagogue, along with other items such as spice boxes, silver goblets, paintings and engravings. But the most unusual exhibit is an enormous glass beaker, made in 1783–4 for the Prague Burial Society and painted with a procession of men and women dressed in funereal black.

➕ 31C2
✉ Maiselova 10, Praha 1
☎ 2481 0099
⏰ Apr–Oct Sun–Fri 9–6, Nov–Mar 9–4:30. Closed Jewish hols
🍴 Restaurant (££) near by
Ⓠ Staroměstská
🚌 Tram 17, 18, bus 135, 207
♿ Few
💲 Moderate
↔ Pinkasova synagóga (➤ 65)

MALOSTRANSKÉ NÁMĚSTÍ (LESSER TOWN SQUARE) ✪

The former market square of the Lesser Town dates from 1257. Looming over the charming ensemble of baroque buildings is St Nicholas's Church and former Jesuit College (➤ 16). Many of the arcaded houses have been converted into cafés and restaurants, making the square an ideal place to linger.

The centrepiece of the square is the attractive Renaissance Town Hall (1617–22) on the eastern side. Next door is the house At the Flavins, with a colourful fresco of the Annunciation.

➕ 30B2
✉ Malostranské náměstí
🍴 Cafés £, restaurants (££–£££)
Ⓠ Malostranská
🚌 12, 22
♿ Few
↔ Chrám Svahéto Mikuláše (➤ 16), Karlův most (➤ 41), Valdštejnský palác (➤ 71)

Did you know ?

A bust on the façade of the Kaiserstein Palace (No 23) honours the famous Czech soprano Ema Destinnová, who worked with the likes of Enrico Caruso, Giacomo Puccini and Richard Strauss in the early 20th century. The house's musical connections go back much further, to the occasion when Mozart heard a performance of Rosetti's Requiem here, led by another famous soprano, Josefína Dusková.

Opposite page: *rooftop view over the crooked backstreets of Prague*

Maltézské náměstí: the square has long been associated with the Knights of Malta

MALTÉZSKÉ NÁMĚSTÍ (MALTESE SQUARE) ✪

This neighbourhood has been associated with the Order of the Knights of Malta since 1169. At the corner of Lázeňská is the former convent of the Order – Maltese crosses can still be seen on the main door and under the roof. Two impresive Gothic towers stand guard over the entrance to the Church of Our Lady Below the Chain, where a painting by Karel Škréta, decorating the main altar, depicts the victory of the Maltese Knights over the Turks at Lepanto in 1571. At the southern end of the square are two grand palaces: the brilliant pink-and-white Palais Turba, now the Japanese Embassy, and the ornate Nostitz Palace (open for chamber music concerts), which belongs to the Dutch Embassy.

MUZEUM BEDŘICHA SMETANY (SMETANA MUSEUM) ✪

The life and work of the 'father of Czech Music', Bedřich Smetana (1824–84), are traced here through letters, documents, scores and musical instruments. Smetana studied piano and composition in Prague, where he heard Liszt and, later, Berlioz perform. A fervent patriot, whose music helped inspire the Czech national revival of the 19th century, he is best known abroad for his emotionally charged symphonic poem, *Ma vlast* (My homeland) – the famous second movement evokes the swirling currents of the Vltava. He also composed some fine chamber music, as well as numerous operas for the National Theatre, including *The Bartered Bride* and *The Kiss*. Smetana's later life was clouded by personal tragedy: in 1874 he went profoundly deaf after suffering from tinitis and later lost his reason, dying in an asylum.

MUZEUM HLAVNÍHO MĚSTA PRAHY (CITY OF PRAGUE MUSEUM)

This interesting museum charts the history of Prague, and includes exhibits which range from the earliest times to the 20th century. Among the various household items on display are slippers, combs and a 14th-century wash-tub, as well as pottery and coins. The medieval craft guilds are represented in displays of tools, signs and seals, and by some fine examples of their workmanship, including a mural painting of 1406, originally executed for the House at the Golden Angel in Old Town Square. Weapons, model soldiers and cannons and the lock of the original Bethlehem Chapel door (► 32) are used to illustrate the Hussite period and there is an impressive collection of statuary, notably a wooden *pietà* from the Týn Church (► 46) and a stone Madonna which used to decorate the Oriel Chapel in the Old Town Hall (► 22). Another attraction is Antonín Langweil's ambitious model of 19th-century Prague, which can be illuminated to show different areas of the city.

www.muzeumkomunismu.cz
✚ 31C2
✉ Savarin Palace, Na Příkopě 10, Praha 1 (first floor, same entrance as Casino)
☎ 2242 12966
🕐 Daily 9–9
Ⓜ Můstek
♿ None 🚻 Cheap

MUZEUM KOMUNISMU (MUSEUM OF COMMUNISM) ✪

As a modern visitor to Prague it's all to easy to forget that for more than 40 years (1948-89) the Czech Republic was an occupied country within the Soviet bloc, a client state adhering to the prevailing Communist ideology. The exhibition 'Dreams, Reality and Nightmare of Communism' is an intriguing introduction to the period through photographs, posters, household ephemera, agricultural machinery, military hardware, replica workshops, shop fronts etc. Every aspect of life under the dictatorship is covered, from agriculture to sport, from the economy to the political police. Highlights include secret archive film of the events leading to the Velvet Revolution and a replica interrogation room from the time of the show trials of the 1950s. The persistent ring of the telephone is a suitably eerie touch.

✚ 31D2
✉ Na poříčí 52, Praha 1
☎ 2248 16772
🕐 Tue–Sun 9–6
🍽 None Ⓜ Florenc
🚌 8, 24
♿ None 🚻 Cheap

Above: *Smetana Museum*

19th-century stained-glass panels illuminate the main staircase in the Muzeum Uměleckoprůmyslové

www.mucha.cz
✚ 31C2
✉ Kaunický palác, Panská 7, Praha 1
☎ 2214 51333
🕐 Daily 10–6
Ⓜ Můstek
🎫 Moderate
↔ Obecní dům (▶ 61), Václavské náměstí (▶ 25)

MUZEUM ALFONSE MUCHY (MUCHA MUSEUM) ✪✪

This new museum allows you an opportunity to discover the work of one of the great masters of art nouveau, Alphonse Mucha (1860–1939). Mucha began his career in 1887, shortly after studying at the Academy of Arts in Munich, when he found work as a set painter and decorator in Vienna and Paris. His most famous early illustrations were the posters designed for the French actress Sarah Bernhardt. He settled in Prague in 1910, having spent several years teaching. Other examples of his work can be seen in Obecní Dům, the National Gallery and the Art and Industry Museum. The collection is a representative cross-section of works from the Mucha Foundation: paintings, drawings, lithographs, pastels, sculptures, photographs and personal memorabilia. The museum shop sells a range of souvenirs with eye-catching Mucha motifs.

✚ 31C3
✉ 17 listopadu 2, Praha 1
☎ 2510 93111
🕐 Tue–Sun 10–6
Ⓜ Staroměstská
🚌 17, 18, 51, 54
♿ Few
🎫 Cheap
↔ Náměstí Jana Palacha (▶ 58), Rudolfinum (▶ 66)

MUZEUM UMĚLECKOPRŮMYSLOVÉ ✪✪
(MUSEUM OF DECORATIVE ARTS)

Once housed in the Rudolfinum, the museum moved to Josef Schulz's neo-Renaissance building in 1901, and boasts a rich collection of Czech and European applied arts. For the time being, only a fraction is on display in the three large halls, but there is plenty to enjoy. The collection of Bohemian glass dates back to the Renaissance and is outstanding, but don't overlook the Venetian and medieval exhibits. There are selections of Meissen and Sèvres porcelain, exquisite majolica tableware from Urbino and Delft and beautifully inlaid cabinets, bureaux and escritoires, from baroque to Biedermeier. The museum shop sells a wide range of art publications and catalogues, as well replicas and souvenirs.

A Walk Around the Castle Grounds

This walk explores the hinterland of Prague Castle, taking in Petřín Hill with its superb views across the city.

Begin at Hradčanské náměstí and head away from the castle.

In the middle of Hradčany Square (➤ 40) is a baroque Plague Column of 1726 and, near by, a wrought-iron street lamp – a relic from the days of gas lighting.

Walk along Loretánská. Turn right at the end to the shrine of the Loreta (➤ 19).

The carillon in the tower first rang out on 15 August 1695 (the Feast of the Assumption of the Virgin). If you happen to be here on the hour, you will hear the 27 bells play a popular hymn tune, *We Greet Thee a Thousand Times*.

Walk back to Loretánská as far as the junction with Pohořelec. Turn right into Pohořelec, past Úzov, then left into the Strahov Monastery (➤ 24).

On your left is the 17th-century Church of St Roch, patron saint of plague victims. Ahead is the Abbey Church of the Annunciation.

Enter the monastery courtyard through the medieval gateway to the left of the church and leave by the arch at the eastern end. Take the downhill path through the Strahov gardens (once the monastic orchards), then climb the steps to your right to the summit of Petřín Hill (➤ 64). Continue the descent by funicular railway to Újezd.

The funicular railway was constructed for the Jubilee Exhibition of 1891 and runs daily 9:15–8:45.

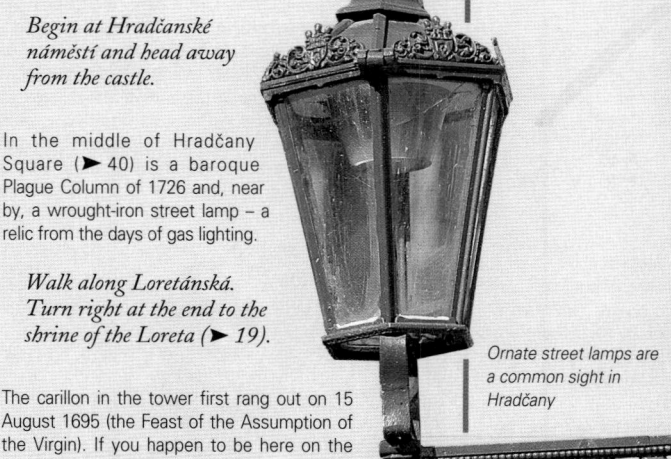

Ornate street lamps are a common sight in Hradčany

Distance
2km

Time
2½ hrs without stops

Start point
Hradčany náměstí
➕ 40B1

End point
Újezd/ Karmelitska
➕ 30B2

Lunch
Saté Grill (£)
✉ Pohořelec 3
☎ 2205 14552

Memorial to the Czech martyr of the Soviet occupation Jan Palach outside the philosophy building of the university where he studied

NÁMĚSTÍ JANA PALACHA (JAN PALACH SQUARE)

'Red Army Square' was renamed after the Velvet Revolution to commemorate Jan Palach, the 21-year-old philosophy student who burnt himself to death in January 1969 as a protest against the Soviet occupation of Czechoslovakia. The authorities were unmoved but more than 800,000 people joined the funeral procession to Olšanské cemetery, where his remains were laid to rest. On the east side of the square is the philosophy building of the university, where Palach attended lectures: on the lower left-hand corner of the façade is a small bronze death mask by Olbran Zoubek.

NA PŘÍKOPĚ (ON THE MOAT)

This busy, pedestrianised street takes its name from the moat which once formed a boundary between the Old and New Towns. Today it is one of Prague's major shopping thoroughfares, with some compelling architecture from the late 19th century, when a number of major banking houses established their offices here. Particularly impressive is No 18–20. Actually two buildings connected by a bridge, it was designed by Osvald Polívka and completed in 1896. The colourful mosaics in the lunettes are from cartoons by the Czech artist, Mikoláš Aleš.

NÁRODNÍ DIVADLO (NATIONAL THEATRE) ✪✪

Partly funded by public donations, the founding of a National Theatre in this striking building overlooking the River Vltava represented the re-emergence of Czech nationalism in the mid-19th century. The foundation stone was laid in 1848 to the accompaniment of folk dancing and celebrations, and when the almost completed theatre was destroyed by fire in 1881, the Czechs immediately began raising more money and finished a second National Theatre in just two years. The design by Josef Schulz closely followed Josef Zítek's original.

The decoration was entrusted to a group of artists who became known as 'the generation of the National Theatre'. The loggia facing Národní has five arcades decorated with lunette paintings by Josef Tulka, while the attic contains statues by Bohuslav Schnirch, Antonín Wagner and Josef Myslbek. The interior is even more resplendent: in the portrait gallery, Myslbek sculpted bronze busts of Smetana and other contributors to Czech opera and drama, and Mikoláš Aleš, Adolf Liebscher and František Ženíšek filled the foyers with paintings. The stage curtain depicting the story of the National Theatre is by Voitěch Hynais.

www.narodnidivadlo.cz
✚ 30B2
✉ Národní 2, Praha 1
☎ 2249 01668
🕐 For concerts
🍴 Café-bar (££)
Ⓜ Národní třída
🚌 6, 9, 17, 18, 22, 51
♿ Few
↔ Betlémská kaple (➤ 32)

The auditorium of the Národní divadlo with a ceiling by František Ženíšek

NÁRODNÍ MUZEUM (NATIONAL MUSEUM) ✪

This stolid neo-Renaissance building, crowned with a gilded dome, dominates Wenceslas Square. Serving up large but unimaginative helpings of natural history, mineralogy, palaentology, zoology and anthropology, the museum is worth visiting for the richly decorated Ceremonial Hall and Pantheon. Statues of famous Czechs compete with historical wall paintings and allegories of Science, Art, Inspiration and Power, all commissioned from Bohemia's best 19th-century sculptors and painters.

www.nm.cz
✚ 31C1
✉ Václavské náměstí 68, Praha 1
☎ 2244 97111
🕐 May–Sep daily 10–6, Oct–Apr daily 9–5. Closed every first Tue
🍴 Café (£)
Ⓜ Muzeum ♿ Few
💰 Moderate

www.ntm.cz
🔲 31C3
✉ Kostelní 42, Praha 7
☎ 2203 99111
🕐 Tue–Fri 9–5, Sat–Sun
10–6
Ⓜ Vltavská, Hradčanská
🚋 1, 8, 25, 26
♿ Few
💵 Cheap
↔ Veletržní palác (➤ 26),
Lapidarium (➤ 51)

*Pilot's-eye view of the
Transport Hall of the
Národní Technické
Muzeum*

🔲 30B3
✉ Nerudova, Praha 1
🍴 Cafés (£), restaurants
(££–£££)
🚋 12, 27, 57
♿ None
💵 Free
↔ Pražský hrad (➤ 20–1),
Chrám Svatého Mikuláše
(➤ 16), Malostranské
náměstí (➤ 53)

*The sign of the house
At the Three Fiddles on
Nerudova*

NÁRODNÍ TECHNICKÉ MUZEUM ⬤⬤
(NATIONAL TECHNICAL MUSEUM)

The vast, glass-roofed central hall is the main attraction of
this museum, with its exhibition on the history of transport,
featuring more than 500 vehicles, machines and models.
Suspended from the ceiling is the skeleton of an early
powered glider dating from 1905 and J Kašpar's Bleriot-XI
monoplane of 1910. A magnificent steam engine and
tender, built in Prague for the Austrian State Railways in
1911, dwarfs everything else in the locomotives exhibition,
and a wonderful collection of early automobiles starts with
an 1893 Benz 'Viktoria'. The Czechs' own Skoda Works are
represented by a wood-upholstered fire engine from 1928.

Among the 40,000 items displayed elsewhere in the
museum are film cameras, clocks and watches, astrolabes,
sextants, phonographs and much else besides. Visits to the
simulated mining gallery are by guided tour only.

NERUDOVA ⬤⬤

This street honours Pavel Neruda (1834–91), whose short
stories capture perfectly the small-town atmosphere of
19th-century Prague, and who was born at No 47. It's a
steep climb to the top – Nerudova was originally called
Spur Street after the
brake which was
applied to coaches on
their descent. On your
way you will see some
wonderful 18th-century
house signs (numbers
were not introduced
until the 1770s). Look
out for The Red Eagle
(No 6), The Three
Fiddles (No 12), The
Golden Cup (No 16),

The Golden Horseshoe (No 34), The Green Lobster (No
43), the Two Suns (No 47) and the White Swan (No 49).
Two magnificent baroque mansions, the Thun Hohenstein

Palace (No 20) and the Morzín Palace (No 5) are now the Italian and Romanian embassies. Nerudova leads eventually to Prague Castle, a wonderful vantage point from which to view the city.

NOVÝ SVĚT (NEW WORLD) ✪

One of the prettiest corners of Hradčany, Nový Svět is a country lane of quaint cottages dating back to the 17th century. Look out for U Zletého noha (At the Golden Griffin, No 1), where the astronomers Tycho Brahe and Johannes Kepler once lived and U Zlaté hrušky (At the Golden Pear, No 3), now one of Prague's finest restaurants.

Homage to Prague by Karel Špillar, mosaic on the façade of Obecní dům

- 🕀 30A3
- ✉ Nový Svět
- 🍴 Restaurant (£££)
- 🚌 22 ♿ Few
- 🚇 None
- ↔ Loreta (► 19), Strahovský klášter (► 24)

OBECNÍ DŮM (MUNICIPAL HOUSE) ✪✪✪

One of Prague's most engaging art nouveau monuments, Obecní dům was conceived as a community centre with concert halls, assembly rooms, offices, cafés and restaurants. Antonín Balšánek and Osvald Polívka won a competition for the design and it was completed in 1911. Each of the rooms has its own character, but there is overall unity in the stained-glass windows, inlaid floors, wrought-iron work and walls of polished wood or marble. Scarcely a Czech artist of the period failed to contribute to the interiors. The Smetana Concert Hall was decorated by Karel Špillar and Ladislav Šaloun; Alfons Mucha was responsible for the Mayor's Salon. Just as remarkable is Špillar's large mosaic, *Homage to Prague*, on the façade.

- www.obecnidum.cz
- 🕀 31C2
- ✉ Náměstí Republiky 5, Praha 1
- ☎ 2220 02127/2220 02101
- 🍴 Café (£), restaurants (£££)
- 🚇 Náměstí Republiky
- 🚌 5, 14, 26
- ♿ Good
- 🚹 Free
- ↔ Celetná (► 34), Na Příkopě (► 58), Prašná brána (► 66)
- ❓ Temporary exhibitions

In the Know

If you only have a short time to visit Prague, or would like to get a real flavour of the city, here are some ideas:

10
Ways To Be A Local

A good sense of humour and a sense of the ridiculous are typical Czech characteristics, so be ready to share a joke.
Sample the atmosphere in a traditional beer bar (*pivnice /hospoda*), like U Zlatého tygra.
Check out the form at the races, there are hurdle and steeplechases, also trotting races ⊠ Velká Chuchle course, Radotínská 69, Praha 5 ☎ 2579 41431.
It's polite to share a table in a crowded restaurant and a good way to get to know Czechs.
Take a short cut through the passageways off Wenceslas Square (➤ 25).
Learn a few words of Czech.

More Praguers are coming to terms with English, but they'll appreciate your efforts.
If you're invited into a Czech home, take some flowers for your hosts.
Don't talk about Communism or the Russians. Many Czechs prefer to forget the occupation. A safer topic of conversation is the much-loved First Republic (the inter-war years).
Take a fast-food lunch with the office workers in the Franciscan Gardens.
Go and watch Prague's leading soccer and ice hockey teams (both called Sparta Praha) at a home game. You can buy their colours from department stores.

10
Good Places To Have Lunch

Café Louvre
⊠ Národní třida 20, Praha 1
☎ 2249 30949.
Upstairs restaurant (non-smoking room) with views of the Art Nouveau architecture on Narodní.
Ethno Café Bar
⊠ Husova 10 ☎ 2232 13713. Ethnic bric-á-brac, including Guatemalan wood carvings, African cane fans and exotic fabric parrots, provides the décor in this pleasant café.

Le Bistro de Marlene
⊠ Plavecká 4, Vyšehrad
☎ 2249 27853. Round off your tour of the ancient fortress with the best French meal in Prague. Open for lunch Mon–Fri 12–2, reservations advisable.
Nebozízek Restaurant
⊠ Petřínské sady
☎ 2573 15329. The food isn't special but the views from the terrace (reached by funicular) are spectacular. Popular, so reserve a table.
Pizzeria Rugantino
⊠ Dusní 4, Praha 1
☎ 2223 18172. Old Town restaurant, serving salads, pies and pizzas cooked in a wood-fired oven.
Slavia Kavárna
⊠ Smetanovo nábřeži /Národní, Praha 1
☎ 2422 18493. Captivating views of the river and Mala Strana make this old fashioned café-restaurant special.
Take a picnic in the small park on Divadelní (near the National Theatre), where there are panoramic views of Prague Castle.
U Kalicha ⊠ Na Bojišti 12 ☎ 2249 16475 Immortalised by Jaroslav Hašek's novel, *The Good Soldier Schweik*, U Kalicha cashes in on the literary connection with mugs and other memorabilia.
U Pešků ⊠ Náměsti Míruq 9. Although catering mainly for Czechs rather than tourists, this traditional restaurant welcomes visitors.

Knedlíky (dumplings) are a common side-dish in Czech restaurants

U Zlatého Stromu
✉ Karlova 6 ☎ 2242 21385. 'At the Golden Tree' is an old hotel with a warm atmosphere. Dishes include Prague toast, chicken salad and pizzas (illustrated menu).

10
Top Activities

Bowling: Bowling Centrum RAN Hotel Marriott) ✉ V Celnici 10, Praha 1 ☎ 2210 33020.
Canoeing: on the Berounka River – experienced canoers and beginners (Saturdays and Sundays), Central European Adventures ✉ Jáchymova 4, Praha 1 ☎ 2223 28879.
Cycling: bikes – and mountain bikes – may be rented from Central European Adventures ✉ Jáchymova 4, Praha 1 ☎ 2223 28879 who arrange bicycle tours to Karlstejn and the Koněprusy Caves, also day trips around Prague. Closed Mondays.
Fitness Centres: Hotel Axa ✉ Na poříčí 40, Praha 1 ☎ 2248 1250; Fitness Club ✉ InterContinental Hotel, Náměstí Curieovych 43/5, Praha 1 ☎ 2966 31111

Golf: There is a challenging 18-hole golf course at Golf Club Praha (behind Hotel Golf) ✉ Plzeňská, Praha 5 ☎ 2572 16584. For something less strenuous the Erpet Golf Centrum offers an 18-hole virtual reality golf course, as well as astro-turf putting greens and driving platforms for some serious practice ✉ Strakonická 510, Praha 5 ☎ 2573 21177.
Jogging: there are plenty of open spaces for running in Prague including Stromovka Park, the Vyšehrad ramparts, around Strahov, Kampa Island and Letna.
Karting: Go-karts are available for hire every day on an individual or group basis from ✉ Hůlkova 16, Praha ☎ 6028 78717.
Sports Centres: swimming, sauna, massage, squash, tennis and bowling are all available at Sportcentrum Hotel, Čechie Praha ✉ U Sluncové 618, Praha 8 ☎ 2661 94111; Clubhotel Praha ✉ Průhonice 400 ☎ 2740 10740.
Swimming: there are indoor and outdoor pools at Podolí ✉ Podolská 74, Praha 4 ☎ 2414 33952 There is also a beach at Džbán Reservoir ✉ Šárka Nature Reserve, Praha 6, with a special section for nude bathing.
Tennis: this is a very popular sport in the Czech Republic and there are

clay courts at Štvanice Lawn Tennis Club ✉ Štvanice Island, Praha 7 ☎ 2223 24601 ✉ Bendvik Diskařskál, Praha 1 ☎ 2205 14015.

5
Things To Do On The River

- Dine on a terrace at the Kampa Park Restaurant ✉ Na Kampě 8b ☎ 2575 32685, overlooking the Vltava.
- Take a pleasure cruise with buffet lunch and live music. EVD, departing from Náměstí Republiky at 11.40AM ☎ 2223 14661
- Take a stroll around the islands: Kampa (Malá Strana), Veslarský ostrov (Podolí), Císařská Louka (Smíchov), Slovanský ostrov Žofín (Nové Město).
- Hire a rowing boat from Rent-A-Boat ✉ Slovanský ostrov (with lanterns at night).
- Feed the waterbirds on the Čertovka river.

5
Views of Prague

- From 'the metronome' on Letna Gardens – there used to be a statue of Stalin here.
- Across the Malá Strana from the Observatory in Petřín Park.
- Along the Vltava River valley from the ramparts of Vyšehrad.
- Spectacular views of the city from the astronomical tower of the Klementínum.
- Across the Staré Město from the tower of the Town Hall.

View from Petřínské sady across the Malá Strana (Lesser Quarter) to Pražský hrad (Prague Castle)

31C3
U Starého hřbitova, Praha 1 ☎ 2248 1485
Apr–Oct Sun–Fri 9–6, Nov–Mar 9–4:30
Staroměstská
17, 18, 135, 207
Moderate
Klausová synagóga (► 44), Starý židovský hřbitov (► 69)

OBŘADNÍ SÍŇ (CEREMONIAL HALL) ✪

Once used for Jewish burial rites, the Ceremonial Hall is now used to exhibit drawings by some of the 15,000 children who were confined at the Terezín concentration camp. There are also poignant poems, school exercises and records left by the adult prisoners, including some fine paintings, sketches, diaries, even music – all reminders that the human spirit cannot be extinguished, even in the face of the most barbaric cruelty.

31C2
Národní třída, Praha 1
Cafés (£), restaurants (££–£££) near by
Národní třída
6, 9, 18, 22, 51
None
Free
Václavské náměstí (► 25), Národní divadlo (► 59)

PAMÁTNÍK 17 LISTOPADU 1989 ✪

In an arcade between Wenceslas Square and the National Theatre is a small plaque commemorating the incident that sparked off the Velvet Revolution in 1989. On 17 November a large crowd, made up predominantly of students, headed towards Wenceslas Square from Vyšehrad, where they had been marking the 50th anniversary of the Nazi occupation. When they reached Národní they were confronted by riot police who charged, leaving hundreds severely beaten. Actors and theatre employees immediately called a strike, which led ultimately to the formation of Civic Forum.

30B2
Petřínské Sady, Hradčany
Tower 2573 2011
All attractions: May–Aug daily 10–10, Apr, Sep 10–7, Oct 10–6, Nov–Mar Sat–Sun 10–5
Restaurant (£££)
Funicular
6, 9, 12, 27, 57
Strahovský klášter (► 24)

PETŘÍNSKÉ SADY (PETŘÍN HILL) ✪✪

Petřín Hill, where pagans once made sacrifices to their gods and medieval monarchs executed their enemies, is today a cool, restful haven with panoramic views of the city. Crowning the summit is the baroque Church of St Lawrence; the ceiling fresco here depicts the founding of an earlier church in 991 on the site of a pagan shrine. The 60m-high Observation Tower, modelled on the Eiffel Tower in Paris, was built for the Jubilee Exhibition of 1891, along with the Mirror Maze and a diorama depicting a battle between the Czechs and the Swedes for control of the Charles Bridge in 1648. Encircling the hill is the Hunger Wall, built in 1360 by Charles IV to provide employment in a time of famine. Lower down the hill, near the funicular stop, is the Observatory and Planetarium.

PINKASOVA SYNAGÓGA
(PINKAS SYNAGOGUE) ✪

First mentioned in 1492, the synagogue was founded by Rabbi Pinkas and enlarged by his great-nephew, Aaron Meshulam Horowitz, in 1535. A women's gallery and an impressive council hall were added in the early 17th century. The synagogue is now a memorial to the Holocaust, the walls painstakingly painted in red and black letters with the names and dates of the 77,297 Bohemian and Moravian Jews who perished in Nazi death camps during World War II. (The original paintings were erased by the Communists when they closed the building in 1968, ostensibly to prevent flood damage.) During recent excavations, a medieval ritual bath and the remains of several wells were discovered in the basement, evidence that there was probably a Jewish place of worship on this site long before the time of Rabbi Pinkas.

➕ 31C3
✉ Široká 3, Praha 1
☎ 2248 1458
🕐 Apr–Oct Sun–Fri 9–6, Nov–Mar 9–4:30. Closed Jewish hols
🍴 Café (£), restaurant (££) near by
Ⓜ Staroměstská
🚌 17, 18, 135, 207
♿ Few ✦ Moderate
↔ Maiselova synagóga (➤ 53), Starý židovský hřbitov (➤ 69)

Did you know?

According to legend, Rabbi Löw (1512–1609) created a golem from clay, water, air and fire. It had superhuman powers which it used to protect Josefov residents from persecutors. The golem gripped the popular imagination and has been the subject of books, films and even an opera, composed by Hanuš Bartoň for Opera Furore in 1992.

The Calvary Chapel near the Observation Tower on Petřínské sady

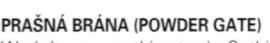

www.cpost.cz
31C3
Nové mlyny 2, Praha 1
2223 12006
Tue–Sun 9–5
Náměstí Republiky
5, 8, 14
None Cheap

Traditional Post Office sign in the Poštovní muzeum

31C2
Náměstí Republiky, Praha 1
Apr–Jun daily 10–5, Jul–Oct 10–10
Náměstí Republiky
5, 14, 26
None
Moderate
Celetná (➤ 34), Na Příkopě (➤ 58), Obecní dům (➤ 61)

The Prašná brána is one of Prague's most familiar landmarks

www.rudolfinum.cz
31C3
Alsovo nábřeží 12, Praha 1
2270 59205
Gallery Tue–Sun 10–6
Staroměstská
17, 18, 51, 54
Gallery: cheap
Muzeum Uměleckprům-yslové (➤ 56), Náměstí Jana Palacha (➤ 58)

POŠTOVNÍ MUZEUM (POSTAL MUSEUM) ✪

A philatelist's delight but of wider appeal, too, this unusual museum boasts a colourful collection of postage stamps from Czechoslovakia, the Czech Republic and Europe. The backdrop is an exhibition on the history of communications in the region, using prints, old signs and other ephemera. There are also temporary exhibitions, for example on the postal service in the time of Rudolph II. The frescos in the showroom are by the 19th-century artist, Josef Navrátil.

PRAŠNÁ BRÁNA (POWDER GATE) ✪✪

Work began on this sturdy Gothic tower, originally the most important of 13 gateways into the Old Town, in 1475, but was halted eight years later when rioting forced the King to flee the city. It still lacked a roof when Josef Mocker was asked to complete it in the 1870s. The gate acquired its name in the 17th century, when it was used to store gunpowder. Before then its functions had been ceremonial: coronation processions began here before moving off towards St Vitus's Cathedral. The tower is a fine vantage point for Old Town views.

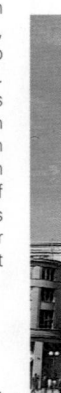

PRAŽSKÝ HRAD (➤ 20–1 TOP TEN)

RUDOLFINUM ✪

One of Prague's leading cultural venues, the Rudolfinum is also a fine example of neo-Renaissance architecture. It was designed by Josef Zítek and Josef Schulz in 1876 and named in honour of the Austrian crown prince, Rudolph of Hapsburg. Concert-goers will come to know the Dvořák Hall, home of the Czech Philharmonic orchestra (chamber concerts and recitals are held in the 'small hall'). The Galerie Rudolfinum is used for contemporary art shows and other events.

A Walk Through the Lesser Quarter

From Malostranská metro station take Valdstejnská to Valdstejnské námestí.

The square is named after the Imperial commander, Albrecht von Valdstein, whose palace straddles the east side (➤ 71). Behind the Ledebour Palace (No 3) are two attractive terraced gardens (open to the public), hugging the slopes below Prague Castle.

Take Tomásská to Malostranské námestí. Walk along the east side of the square to Karmelitska.

Before crossing to Malostranské námestí, stop to admire Dientzenhoffer's baroque church, St Thomas's (➤ 48). The lower part of the square was once the site of a gallows and pillory. Now café tables spill out onto the pavement outside the Town Hall.

Leave the square by Karmelitska and continue past Trzište to the Church of Our Lady Victorious (➤ 46) which contains the celebrated statue of Il Bambino di Praga.

On the corner of Trzište you pass the Vrtba Palace, which has a delightful terraced garden, constructed around 1720.

Cross Karmelitska and turn left down Harantova. Walk through Maltézké námestí (➤ 54) and turn right onto Velkoprevorské námestí, which leads down to the river.

Beyond the Lennon Wall (➤ 51) and the approach to the Vltava is a little bridge crossing the Čertovka (Devil's Stream). On your left is the waterwheel of the Grand Prior's Mill, which, in common with much of the area, belonged to the Order of the Knights of Malta.

Turn right and follow the river to most Legii, where you can catch a tram back to the centre.

Journey into the past: the picturesque Čertovka (Devil's Stream) waterwheel in the Malá Strana (Lesser Quarter)

Distance
2km

Time
2hrs without stops

Start point
Malostranská
30B3

End point
Most Legii
30B2
6, 9, 22, 57, 58

Lunch
U Mecenášo (£££)
Malostranské námestí 10
2275 31631

STAROMĚSTSKÁ RADNICE (► 22 TOP TEN)

STAROMĚSTSKÉ NÁMĚSTÍ ✪✪✪
(OLD TOWN SQUARE)

As early as the 12th century Old Town Square was a thriving market place. Merchants from all over Europe conducted their business here and in the Ungelt (► 71), a courtyard behind the Týn Church. The square was also a place of execution: among the victims were the Hussite rebel Jan Želivský and the 27 Protestant noblemen who died here following the Battle of the White Mountain in 1620 (they are commemorated by white crosses set in the pavement in front of Old Town Hall). Jan Hus, the father of Czech Protestantism, died in Constance, but his monument, a stark sculpture by Ladislav Šaloun (1915), stands in the centre of the square.

Today Old Town Square is primarily a place of entertainment where buskers and street traders vie with circus acts and side-shows, and the Astronomical Clock on the Old Town Hall (► 22) performs its mesmerising hourly routine. But the square's chief glory is its architecture: the Renaissance and baroque façades of the houses, painted in pastel shades, conceal Gothic substructures and Romanesque cellars; many are decorated with sculpted house signs and other emblems. The beautiful rococo embellishments on the Golz-Kinsky Palace, dating from 1765 (No 12 east side) are by Kilian Dientzenhofer. Franz Kafka went to school here in the 1890s. Directly in front of the Týn Church, the ribbed vaulting in the 14th-century Týn School arcade has survived.

Renaissance sgraffito covers the façade of the house At the Minute in Staroměstské náměstí

STARONOVÁ SYNAGÓGA
(OLD-NEW SYNAGOGUE)

😀😀😀

Founded around 1270, the Old-New Synagogue is the oldest in northern Europe and is still open for worship. A typical Gothic building with a double nave, its most unusual feature is the five-ribbed vaulting of the main hall, unique in Bohemian architecture. Other details to look out for are the stepped brick gables on the exterior, the grape clusters and vine leaf motifs above the entrance portal and the medieval furnishings, including stone pews. There are 13th-century Gothic carvings in the tympanum above the Holy Ark, and the iron lattice enclosing the *almenor* or *bimah* (the tribune from where the Torah is read) dates from the late 15th century. Suspended between two of the pillars is a large red flag embroidered with the Star of David and the traditional Jewish cap. It was presented to the community in 1648 by the Emperor Ferdinand in appreciation of its contribution to the Thirty Years' War.

- ✚ 31C3
- ✉ Červená, Pařížská, Praha 1
- ☎ 2248 1485
- 🕐 Apr–Oct Sun–Thu 9–6, Fri 9–5, Nov–Mar Sun–Thu 9–4:30, Fri 9–2. Closed Jewish hols
- 🍴 Restaurant (££) near by
- Ⓜ Staroměstská
- 🚌 17, 18, 135, 207
- ♿ None 💰 Moderate
- ↔ Josefov (► 17)

STARÝ ŽIDOVSKÝ HŘBITOV
(OLD JEWISH CEMETERY)

😀😀😀

One of the oldest Jewish burial grounds in Europe, the Old Jewish cemetery was founded in the early 15th century: the earliest grave, belonging to Rabbi Avigdor Kara, dates from 1439. There are approximately 12,000 tombstones sprouting obliquely from the earth like so many broken and decaying teeth. Beneath them lie more than 100,000 bodies, buried layer upon layer in the confined space. The cemetery closed in 1787. This was the last resting place of many prominent members of the Jewish community, including Rabbi Jehuda Löw (1609), legendary inventor of the Golem (► 65), the mayor and philanthropist, Mordechai Maisel (1601) and the renowned scholar, Rabbi David Openheim (1736). The earliest headstones are of sandstone and have plain inscriptions, but from the 17th century they are decorated with carved marble reliefs indicating the trade or status of the deceased – for example, a pair of scissors for a tailor.

- ✚ 31C3
- ✉ U Starého hřbitova, Praha 1
- ☎ 2248 1458
- 🕐 Apr–Oct Sun–Fri 9–6, Nov–Mar 9–4:30. Closed Jewish hols
- Ⓜ Staroměstská
- 🚌 17, 18, 135, 207
- ♿ None 💰 Moderate
- ↔ Klausenova synagóga (► 44), Obřadní síň (► 64), Pinkasova synagóga (► 65)

Splendid Gothic backdrop of the Staronová synagóga in Josefov

69

www.narodnidivadlo.cz
🚹 31C2
✉ Ovocny trh 1, Praha 1
☎ 2242 15001
🕐 For concerts
🍴 Café (££)   Ⓜ Můstek
♿ None   💷 Free
🚇 Karolinum (▶ 41)

*The restored auditorium
of the celebrated
Stavovské divadlo*

STAVOVSKÉ DIVADLO (ESTATES THEATRE) ⭐⭐

This famous theatre was built in 1781–3 for Count FA Nostitz-Rieneck, who wanted to raise the cultural profile of the city. Only four years later, on 29 October 1787, the count had his wish when Mozart's opera *Don Giovanni* received its world premiere here after being rejected by the more conservative Viennese theatre managers. 'The people of Prague understand me', the composer is reported to have said after conducting the performance from the piano. In 1984 Miloš Forman shot the relevant scenes of his Oscar-winning film *Amadeus* in the auditorium, drawing attention to the need for renovation. That work was completed in the 1990s.

🚹 Off map 31D3
✉ U trojského zámku 1, Praha 7
☎ 2838 51614
🕐 Apr–Oct Tue–Sun 10–6, Nov–Mar Sat–Sun 10–5
🚌 112 from Nádraží Holešovice
♿ Few
💷 Moderate

TROJSKÝ ZÁMEK (TROJA CHÂTEAU) ⭐⭐

Count Wenceslas Šternberg cut a swathe through the royal hunting grounds in order to build his version of Versailles at Stromovka. Work began on the striking red-and-white château around 1679. The palace itself is modelled on an Italian villa, but after the death of the original architect, responsibility for the project passed into the hands of a Frenchman, Jean-Baptiste Mathey. To honour the architect's intentions, it is necessary to approach the château from the south, where the formal French garden, restored in the 1980s, leads to an elaborate staircase decorated with heroic statues representing the 'gigantomachia' – the epic struggle between the Gods of

Olympus and the Titans. The château apartments now house 19th-century Czech paintings. Most of the ceiling paintings are by an Italian artist, Francesco Marchetti, but for the Grand Hall, the count turned to the Flemish painter, Abraham Godyn. His frescos are Šternberg's effusive tribute to his Hapsburg masters, notably Leopold I, whose triumph over the Ottomans at the gates of Vienna is symbolised by a Turk tumbling from the painting.

The southern approach to Trojský zámek, built by the Šternbergs in the 17th century

UNGELT ✪✪

In the Middle Ages this courtyard behind the Týn Church was a centre of commerce, where merchants paid *ungelt*, or customs duties. There was also a hostel for travellers here. The complex of 18 buildings dates from the 16th century onwards and has been restored as shops, hotels and offices. The Granovský House, built for a wealthy tax collector in 1560, is one of the most distinguished Renaissance buildings in Prague, with sgraffito depicting biblical and classical themes and a magnificent loggia.

- 🏛 31C2
- ✉ Týnský dvůr, Praha 1
- 🍴 Restaurant in Hotel Ungelt (£££); others (££)
- 🚇 Staroměstská
- ♿ Good
- ↔ Kostel Svatého Jakuba (➤ 47), Staroměstské náměstí (➤ 68)

VÁCLAVSKÉ NÁMĚSTÍ (➤ 25 TOP TEN)

VALDŠTEJNSKÝ PALÁC A SADY (WALLENSTEIN PALACE AND GARDENS) ✪✪

The Imperial General, Albrecht of Wallenstein (1583–1634), was a swashbuckling figure who amassed a tremendous fortune before succumbing to a blow from the assassin's axe. High-walled gardens were laid out in front of the palace by Niccolo Sebregondi between 1624 and 1630. The ceiling of the triple-arched *salla terrena*, designed in the Italian Renaissance style by Giovanni Pieronni, is decorated with scenes from the Trojan Wars. An avenue of bronze sculptures by Adam de Vries leads from the pavilion (these are copies: the originals were taken by the Swedes during the Thirty Years' War). At the far end of the garden is the Riding School, now an exhibition hall.

- 🏛 30B3
- ✉ Valdštejnské náměstí, Praha 1
- ☎ 5132 4545
- 🕐 Apr–Oct daily 10–6
- 🚇 Malostranská
- 🚌 12, 22
- ♿ Few
- 🎟 Free
- ↔ Chrám Svatého Mikuláše (➤ 16), Malostranské náměstí (➤ 53)

VELETRŽNÍ PALÁC (➤ 26 TOP TEN)

www.morsky-svet.cz
🗓 31D3
✉ Výstaviště-Holešovice,
   Praha 7
☎ 2201 03275/03305
🕐 Daily 10–7
🍴 Café (£), restaurant (££)
   near by
🚇 Holešovice
♿ Good
💲 Moderate
↔ Veletržní Palac (➤ 26)

The rooftops and buildings of Nove Mesto (New Town), laid out in the 14th century, viewed from the hilltop site of the ancient High Castle or Vysehrad, on the east bank of the Vltava

www.praha-vysehrad.cz
🗓 Off map 30B1
✉ Soběslavova 1, Praha 2
🕐 Museum, cemetery:
   Apr–Oct daily 9:30–6,
   Nov–Mar 9:30–5
🍴 Café (£), restaurant (££)
🚇 Vyšehrad
♿ Few
💲 Free

Opposite: *former artisans' cottages in Zlatá ulička, by Pražský hrad (Prague Castle)*

VYŠEHRAD ⊛⊛

Rising from a rocky hill above the River Vltava, the twin spires of Vyšehrad church are one of Prague's best known landmarks (the name means 'castle on the heights'). The early history of this ancient settlement is almost inseparable from the myths and legends surrounding the first dynasty of Czech rulers, the Přemyslids, who established a fortress on the rocky outcrop in the middle of the 10th century. Prince Vratislav II (1061–92) chose this as his residence and built a walled palace, the Basilica of St Peter and St Paul and a chapter house. It was at this time that the foundations were laid of St Martin's Rotunda, one of the oldest Christian buildings in Bohemia. By the mid-12th century, Prague

Castle began to take precedence, but Vyšehrad's value as a stronghold was recognised by Charles IV, who reinforced the walls and (to emphasise his links with the Přemyslids) made this the start of his coronation procession.

Near the remains of the Gothic 'Špička' Gate (nicknamed 'spikey' for its flamboyant decoration) is an information office and café. The elaborate Leopold Gate of 1670 leads into the main compound. Past St Martin's Rotunda is the Old Deanery, which stands on the site of a Romanesque basilica – the foundations are open to the public. Little remains of the early palaces, although from the terrace on the fortified walls there are views of 'Libuše's bath', actually a Gothic guard tower, as well as splendid vistas across the Vltava Valley. In the middle of the palace gardens is a medieval well – the statues by Josef Myslbek were removed from the Palacky Bridge after being damaged during a bombardment in 1945. The Church of St Peter and St Paul has been rebuilt many times, most recently in neo-Gothic style by Josef Mocker. In a side chapel is a medieval panel painting of the Virgin of the Rains, dating from 1350. Vyšehrad cemetery was founded in 1860 as a burial ground for Czech national heroes: the composers Antonín Dvořák and Bedřich Smetana, the artist Alfons Mucha and the writer Karel Čapek are all buried here.

VÝSTAVÍŠTĚ – MORSKY SVET (EXHIBITION GROUND – SEAWORLD) ✪✪

The Exhibition Ground in Letná Park dates from 1891 and is worth a look if only to admire the splendid art nouveau pavilions built for the imperial jubilee of that year. The real tourist attraction though is Seaworld, a vast (1,000sq m) exhibition space devoted to the life of the deep. There are 50 tanks, containing more than 150 species of salt and freshwater fish from all over the world and a spectacular, 25-m long coral cave, constructed with American help in 2003. State-of-the-art technology replicates the natural environment with specially sensitised lighting, while microprocessor-driven water pumps simulate high and low tides.

The ceremonial Leopold Gate at Vyšehrad, commemorating the Austrian Emperor

ZLATÁ ULIČKA (GOLDEN LANE) ✪✪

This row of colourful little cottages, built hard against the walls of Prague Castle, originally provided homes for the archers of the Castle Guard. During the 17th century the palace goldsmiths moved into the area, giving the street its present name. Golden Lane gradually fell into decline and was little better than a slum when Franz Kafka was living with his sister at No 22 during the winter of 1916–17. Today souvenir shops have taken over the repainted houses, attracting crowds of sightseers.

➕ 41F2
✉ Zlatá Ulička , Pražský hrad
🕐 Apr–Oct daily 9–5, Nov–Mar 9–4
🍴 Cafés (£)
Ⓜ Malostranská
🚌 22　♿ None
↔ Pražský hrad (▶ 20–1), Klášter Svatého Jiří (▶ 43)

Excursions

There are any number of possible excursions from Prague, many within an hour or two's journey by train or car. The variety of scenery may come as a surprise, from the craggy uplands of Český Ráj and the Krkonože (Giant) Mountains to the woodland slopes of the Berounka Valley. Further south around Třeboň is a wetland area of lakes and carp-rearing ponds, an ideal habitat for water birds; and there are other surprises in store: a fairy-tale castle on an isolated hill top, a gloomy limestone cave with dripping stalactites, a charming Renaissance town hall at the centre of a busy market square. The elegant 19th-century resort of Karlovy Vary is famous for its hot mineral springs; Plzeň and České Budějovice are both centres of the brewing industry, and the vineyards of Mělník date back to the reign of Charles IV.

' It was the place where the spirit could soar up to any heights, but it was also the place where there was in the atmosphere a barely perceptible smell of decay...'

IVAN KLÍMA,
Love and Garbage (1986)

Left: *Karlštejn Castle was a medieval stronghold of the Bohemian Kings*

www.c-budejovice.cz
+ 77D1
✉ Informační služba,
   Radnická 8
☎ (542) 173 590
🕐 Town Hall: Apr–Sep daily
   9–5. Castle: Tue–Sun 9–5
🍴 Cafés (£), restaurants (££)
🚉 Praha Hlavní Nádraží
♿ Few
💷 Cheap
❓ Aug/Sep: International
   Motorcycling
   Championship

BRNO ★★

The capital of Moravia and the second city of the Republic, Brno is famous for its Motorcycle Grand Prix and trade fairs, but it is also a lively cultural centre with several theatres (including the Reduta, where Mozart conducted his own compositions in 1767) and a number of interesting historical sights. Two Brno landmarks – the Špilberk fortress, which for centuries served as a Hapsburg prison and is now the city museum, and the Gothic Cathedral of St Peter and St Paul – stand on adjacent hills. Below the cathedral is the Old Town. It's worth climbing the tower of the Old City Hall for the views. Notice the middle turret of the hall's Gothic portal, which is askew: according to the local legend, it was left deliberately crooked by the builder as an act of revenge on the burghers for not paying his wages in full.

The fruit and vegetable market, one of the more colourful sights in Brno

THE CZECH REPUBLIC

0   20   40   60   80   100 km

Harrachov
▲1602m
Sněžka
Krkonoše
Vrchlabí
Trutnov
Náchod
Nové Město
nad Metují
Chlum
**Hradec
Králové**
Labe
Pardubice
Chrudim
Litomyšl
Orlické bory
Jeseník
Hrubý Jeseník
1491m
Praděd
Morava
Krnov
Sumperk
Sternberk
Svitavy
Nízký Jeseník
Opava
Ostrava
Karviná
Havířov
Havlíčkův
Brod
Žďar nad
Sázavou
Moravská
M o r a v i a
Olomouc
Odra
Nový Jičín
Frýdek-Místek
Prostějov
Valašské
Meziříčí
Západné Beskydy
Jihlava
Pernstejn
Punkevni
jeskyne
Přerov
vrchovina
Vyškov
Rožnov pod
Radhoštěm
Lešná
Vsetín
Třebíč
Svratka
Moravský
kras
Kroměříž
Javorníky
Žilina
Brno
Slavkov
Zlín
Váh
Jaroměřice
nad Rokytnou
**Uherské
Hradiště**
Martin ■
Vranov
Znojmo
Mikulov
Hodonin
Morava
Strážnice
Bílé Karpaty
Trenčín
SK
Dyje
Lednice
Břeclav
Bratislava
Piešťany

PL

Right: *dramatic overview of Český Krumlov and the River Vltava from the castle*

Below: *detail from the Samson fountain in České Budějovice*

www.c-budejovice.cz

☩ 76C1

✉ Informační centrum: náměstí Přemysla Otakara II 2

☎ (386) 801 413. Brewery: (387) 705 111

🕐 Brewery: daily 9–3, for group tours

🍴 Cafés (£), restaurants (££)

🚆 Praha Hlavní Nádraží

♿ Few

↔ Český Krumlov (➤ 79), Třeboň (➤ 90)

❓ Aug: International Agricultural Show

ČESKÉ BUDĚJOVICE ✪✪

This sedate old town was founded in 1265 by King Otokar II Přemysl as a base from which to attack his enemies, the unruly Vítkovec clan. During the Hussite Wars the mainly German population remained royalist and stoutly defended the Catholic cause. Commercially, the 16th century was a golden age as České Budějovice exploited its precious silver deposits, but the economic and social dislocation caused by the Thirty Years' War put paid to this prosperity and in 1641 the town was ravaged by a terrible fire which damaged or destroyed almost every building of importance. This led to large-scale reconstruction, which accounts for the mainly baroque appearance of today's town. The advent of the railways in the 19th century brought industry to the region and České Budějovice became the third largest city in the country after Prague and Plzeň. Today it is best known for its beer.

The town's main square, náměstí Přemysla Otakara II, is one of the largest in Europe: the Town Hall, a graceful building dating from 1727–30, the 13th-century Church of St Nicholas and the lofty Černá Věž (Black Tower) are the main attractions. It's a climb of 360 steps to the Tower's viewing gallery, but well worth it. A few minutes' walk away is the old meat market (Masné krámy), dating from 1564, now serving as a traditional beer hall. Visitors who develop a taste for Budvar may like to sign up for a tour of the famous brewery.

ČESKÝ KRUMLOV ✪✪✪

Český Krumlov is simply ravishing. Surrounded by rolling countryside and the wooded Šumava Hills, the old town – a UNESCO World Heritage Site – nestles in a bend of the Vltava River. For more than 600 years its fortunes were inseparable from those of the aristocratic families residing in the castle: the lords of Krumlov, the Rožmberks, the Eggenbergs and finally the Schwarzenbergs, who were not dispossessed until after World War II. The castle is part medieval fortress, part château, magnificently set on a clifftop overlooking the town, and boasting a unique bridge resembling an aqueduct, a picture gallery and the oldest private theatre in Europe. Guided tours include a visit to the Hall of Masks, a ballroom painted in 1748 with *trompe-l'oeil* figures of guests attending a masquerade. The houses of the Latrán, the area around the castle, were originally occupied by servants and court scribes. Buildings here include a 14th-century Minorite Monastery and the Eggenberg Brewery, which still makes its deliveries by horse and cart. Below the castle steps is the medieval former hospice and Church of St Jošt, recently converted into private apartments.

The nucleus of the town is on the opposite bank of the Vltava. Prominent on Náměstí Svornosti (the main square) is the Town Hall, with attractive arcades and vaulting. Vilém of Rožmberk is buried in the Gothic Church of St Vítus, which dates from 1439. The Latin School, now a music school and the former Jesuit College, now the Hotel Růže, are also worth a look.

www.ckrumlov.cz

✚ 76B1

✉ Infocentrum: náměstí Svornosti 1

☎ (380) 711 183

🕐 Castle: Apr–May, Sep–Oct Tue–Sun 9–12, 1–4, Jul–Aug 9–12, 1–5
Tower: Apr–Oct Tue–Sun 9–6

🍴 Cafés (£), restaurants (££)

🚆 Praha Hlavní Nádraží (via České Budějovice)

♿ None

♿ Moderate

↔ České Budějovice (► 78), Třeboň (► 90)

❓ Mid–Jun: Five-Petal Rose Festival, Aug: International Music Festival

Above: *an extraordinary multi-tiered bridge crosses the ravine in Český Krumlov*

A Drive Around the Bohemian Uplands

Distance
131km

Time
8 hrs

Start/end point
Prague, Střížkov
✚ 76C3

Lunch
U Tomáše (£)
✉ Náměstí Miru 30, Melnik
☎ (206) 627 357

Leave Prague, heading northwards on highway 608 to Boďanovice, then take highway 9 through Libeznice.

Crossing the River Labe, there are views of the vineyards which cluster around the delightful hillltop town of Mělník (► 86).

Continue on highway 9 to Dubá.

On your way you will pass through Liběchov, which has a château dating from 1730.

Turn left onto the 260 to Úštěk.

The ruins of Hrádek Castle will appear on your left as you approach Úštěk. This charming town posseses an attractive elongated square of Gothic and Renaissance houses, as well as the 'birds' cottages' built like nests on rocky promontories by Italian navvies who constructed the railway in the mid-19th century.

Leave Úštěk on highway 260, travelling northwards.

This scenic route crosses the forested Central Bohemian Heights (České středohoří), a designated area of natural beauty.

Cultivating the hops in the beer-producing region of West Bohemia

At Malé Březno turn left onto highway 261.

The road now tracks between the River Labe and its sandstone cliffs to the industrial town of Ústí nad Labem. On a promontory south of Ústí you will pass Střekov Castle, with its round Gothic tower. It is said to have been the inspiration for Richard Wagner's opera *Tannhäuser*.

Continue on the 261.

Drive through the orchards and hop gardens of the Labe Valley to Litoměřice, an attractive medieval market town with two town halls (Gothic and Renaissance) as well as numerous baroque churches and town houses.

Cross the river and join highway E55 through Terezín (► 90) to return to Prague.

ČESKÝ ŠTERNBERK ⭐⭐

Founded in 1242 on a sheer cliff above the Sázava River, the fortress home of the Šternberk family commands wonderful views of the valley. In 1660–70 the castle was remodelled in the baroque style by Italian craftsmen. The rococo Chapel of St Sebastian and the Yellow Room, with an elaborate stucco moulding by Carlo Bentano, are particularly beautiful. There is also a display of silver miniatures and a set of engravings on the staircase which depict scenes from the Thirty Years' War.

🞤 76C2
✉ Český Šternberk
☎ (317) 855 101
🕓 Jul–Sep Tue–Sun 9–6, May Sat–Sun 9–4, Jun, Oct Tue–Sun 9–5, Nov–Mar Sat–Thu 9–4
🍴 Restaurant (££)
🚌 Bus from Roztyly metro
♿ None 🚻 Moderate

HRADEC KRÁLOVÉ ⭐

Hradec Králové has been the regional capital of Eastern Bohemia since the 10th century. A Husssite stronghold in the 15th century, the town later featured in the Austro-Prussian war of 1866 as the site of the Battle of Königgrätz. At the heart of the old town is an attractive square (actually triangular in shape) known as Žižkovo náměstí after the Hussite warrior, Jan Žižka, who is buried here. Overlooking the square is the gauntly austere 14th-century Cathedral of the Holy Spirit. The free-standing belfry (71.5m high) is known, rather misleadingly, as the White Tower, and was added later. Just in front of the tower is a handsome Renaissance town hall. The Jesuit Church of the Assumption, on the southern side of the square, has an attractive 17th-century interior. Two leading art nouveau architects, Osvald Polívka and Jan Kot, worked in Hradec Králové. Polívka designed the Gallery of Modern Art, which has a superb collection of 20th-century Czech painting, while Kot was responsible for the Regional Museum of East Bohemia just outside the Old Town.

🞤 77D3
✉ Hradec Králové
☎ Information: (495) 534 482
🕓 Museum and Gallery: Tue–Sun 9–12, 1–5
🍴 Cafés (£), restaurants (££)
🚉 Praha hlavní Nádraží
♿ None
❓ Information centre: Gočárova třída 1225

The magnificent medieval fortress of Český Šternberk

www.karlovyvary.cz
✚ 76A3
✉ Lázeňská 1
☎ (353) 224 097
🍴 Cafés (£), restaurants (££–£££)
🚌 Coach from Praha Florenc
♿ Good
❓ May: opening of Spa Season; Jul: International Film Festival

KARLOVY VARY ✪✪

According to legend, Charles IV was out hunting one day when one of his hounds tumbled into a hot spring and the secret of Karlovy Vary was out. In 1522 Dr Payer of Loket set out the properties of the waters in a medical treatise and their fame began to spread. By the end of the 16th century there were more than 200 spa buildings – but the town's present appearance dates mainly from the 19th, when celebrities taking the waters included Beethoven, Chopin, Freud, Karl Marx and Goethe (who came 13 times).

There are 12 hot mineral springs in all, housed in five colonnades. The best known (and the hottest) is the Vřídlo, at 72°C, which spurts to a height of 10m. The wrought-iron Sadová and the neo-Renaissance Mlýnská colonnades preserve something of their 19th-century atmosphere.

Karlovy Vary comes alive in the summer, when there are concerts, theatrical events and festivals. The forested hillsides around the Teplá Valley are ideal for walks; the less energetic may prefer a gentle stroll along the promenade (Stará Louka).

Besides the curative waters, Karlovy Vary is famous for another, more potent liquid: a herb liquer called Becherovka after the doctor who invented the recipe while working at the spa in the early 1700s.

www.hradkarlstejn.cz
✚ 76B2
✉ Karlštejn
☎ (311) 681 617
🕐 May, Jun, Sep daily 9–12, 12:30–5, Jul–Aug daily 9–12, 12:30–6, Oct, Apr daily 9–12, 1–4, Mar, Tue–Sun 9–12, 1–3, Nov–Dec 9–12, 1–3.
🍴 Cafés (£), restaurants (££) near by
🚌 Karlštejn from Praha-Smíchov
♿ None
💰 Expensive
🔄 Křivoklát (➤ 83)
❓ Guided tour only

KARLŠTEJN ✪

Perched on a cliff above the Berounka River, Karlštejn was founded by Charles IV in 1348 as a treasury for the imperial regalia and his collection of relics. In the 19th century the fortress was remodelled in neo-Gothic style by Joseph Mocker. Rooms open to the public include the wood-panelled Audience Hall, the Luxembourg Hall and the Church of Our Lady, which has a fine timber ceiling and fragments of 14th-century fresco painting. The magnificent Chapel of the Holy Cross in the Great Tower (closed for restoration) contains copies of 14th-century panels by Master Theodoric (the originals are in St George's Convent (➤ 43). The walls of the chapel are inlaid with over 2,000 semi-precious stones.

Taking the waters at Karlovy Vary. The distinctive spouted cup is de rigueur

KONOPIŠTĚ ⭐

In 1887 Konopiště Castle was acquired by the heir to the Hapsburg throne, Franz Ferdinand, for his Czech wife Sophie Chotek. The Archduke's abiding passion was hunting – in a career spanning 40 years he bagged more than 300,000 animals. Some of the trophies line the walls of the Great Hall. Also worth seeing is Franz Ferdinand's impressive collection of medieval arms and armour and the landscaped garden with peacocks grazing on the lawn.

www.konopiste.com
- ✚ 76C2
- ✉ Konopiště ☎ (317) 721 36
- ⏰ May–Aug Tue–Sun 9–12, 1–5. Check for rest of year
- 🍴 Restaurant (£)
- 🚉 Benešov from Praha-Smíchov, then bus
- 💷 Expensive
- ❓ Guided tour only

KŘIVOKLÁT ⭐⭐

This beautiful 13th-century castle, with its unusual 35m-high round tower, was once the royal hunting lodge of Charles IV. Inside is the vaulted King's Hall, a Gothic chapel with a fine carved altarpiece, a dungeon once used as a prison and now home to a grim assortment of torture instruments, and the Knights' Hall, with a collection of late Gothic paintings and sculptures.

www.krivoklat.cz
- ✚ 76B3
- ✉ Křivoklát
- ☎ (313) 558 440
- ⏰ Jul–Aug daily 9–12, 1–5, Jun Tue–Sun 9–12, 1–5, May, Sep Tue–Sun 9–12, 1–4, Oct, Apr Tue–Sun 9–12, 1–3, Mar, Nov–Dec Sat–Sun 9–12, 1–3
- 🚉 Křivoklát from Praha-Smíchov, change at Beroun
- ♿ None
- 💷 Moderate
- ↔ Karlštejn (➤ 83)
- ❓ Guided tour only

> ### *Did you know ?*
>
> *Franz Ferdinand is a classic case of the hunter hunted. On 28 June 1914, while on a state visit to Sarajevo in Bosnia, the Archduke and his wife were gunned down by a Serb nationalist.*
> *Within six weeks Europe was at war.*

Classical elegance – the Mlýnská kolonáda at Karlovy Vary

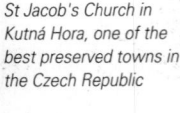

St Jacob's Church in Kutná Hora, one of the best preserved towns in the Czech Republic

 76C2

 Information: Palackeho náměstí 377

 (327) 512 378

 Italian Court: Nov–Feb daily 10–3.30, Mar, Oct daily 10–4.30, Apr, Sep 9–5.30. St Barbara's Cathedral: Nov–Mar Tue–Sun 9–12, 2–3.30, Apr, Oct Tue–Sun 9–12,1–4, May–Sep Tue–Sun 9–5.30 . Museum Hrádek: Apr, Oct Tue–Sun 9–5, May–Sep Tue–Sun 9–6. Ossuary: Nov–Mar daily 9–12, 1–4, Apr–Sep daily 8–12, 1–6

 Cafés (£), restaurants (££–£££)

 Praha Masarykovo to Sedlec, then bus

 Coach from Praha Želivského metro station

 Few

 Jun: international guitar competition

KUTNÁ HORA ★★★

The name means 'mining mountain', and it was the discovery of large deposits of silver and copper ore in the 13th century which turned Kutná Hora overnight into one of the boom towns of Central Europe. A royal mint, founded at the beginning of the 14th century and known as the Italian Court, after Wenceslas II's Florentine advisors, produced its distinctive silver coin, *Pražské grosé*, until 1547. Visitors to the Court can see art nouveau frescos in the Wenceslas Chapel, as well as treasures from the Gothic Town Hall, which burned down in 1770, including a brightly painted wooden statue of Christ, *Ecce Homo* (1502). The Cathedral of St Barbara was endowed by the miners and dedicated to their patron saint. Petr Parléř's unusual design of three tent-roofed spires supported by a forest of flying buttresses was begun in 1388 but not completed until the end of the 15th century, when Matthias Rejsek and Benedikt Reid built the magnificent vaulted ceiling. Colourful frescos in the side chapels show the miners at work. Behind the town museum in Hrádek is a medieval mine where visitors are shown the *trejv*, a horse-drawn winch used for lifting the bags of ore.

North of Kutná Hora is Sedlec, where, in the 19th century, the Cistercian ossuary was turned into a macabre work of art by František Rint. There are bone monstrances, chandeliers and even a Schwarzenberg coat of arms.

A Drive Through the Berounka Valley

Take highway 4 south from Prague towards Stakonice. At Lehovice turn onto the 115 to Revnice (birthplace of tennis champion, Martina Navrátilová). Take the right fork onto the 116 to Karlštejn.

The main attraction here is the Gothic castle perched high above the church. You can also enjoy strolling through the village or sipping a glass of the local wine at one of the terrace bars by the river.

From Karlštejn church take the side road south (away from the castle) then the right fork at Korno, turning right again at Tobolka. Take the next left onto highway 114 to Koněprusy.

The village is famous for its 800m-long network of limestone caves, rich in stalagmites and stalactite formations. There is also an exhibition of finds, including human and animal bones and a clandestine illegal 15th-century mint. Open to the public Apr–Oct Tue–Sun.

Leaving Koněpruské caves, return along the 114, crossing the E50 to Beroun. From Beroun take highway 116 heading northwest along the Berounka Valley.

The river meanders through the Křivoklátsko, an area of dense forest and limestone buffs (now a UNESCO biosphere preservation area).

At Luby, turn left onto the 201, which winds round to the sleepy village of Křivoklát.

Křivoklát Castle (► 83) dates from the late 13th century and, although there have been some alterations to the structure over the years, the Gothic interiors are worth seeing.

Returning along the 201, turn left onto highway 236, leading out of the Křivolátsko at Lany. Turn onto highway 6 (E48) and head east for Prague.

Distance
130km

Time
6 hrs

Start point
Smíchov, Prague
✚ 76C3

End point
Břevnov, Prague
✚ 76C3

Lunch
Hotel Mlyn
✉ 267 27 Karlštejn
☎ (311) 744 411

Tranquil scene on the banks of the Berounka River

85

www.lidice-memorial.cz
✚ 76B3
✉ 10 Června 1942, Lidice
☎ (312) 253 063
🕐 Apr–Sep 9–6, Oct–Mar 9–4
🚌 Bus (Kladno line) from Dejvická metro station
♿ Few
💷 Cheap
❓ 10 Jun: memorial day

Photo montage of the men from Lidice, massacred by the Nazis in 1942

LIDICE ✪

In June 1942, following the assassination of the Nazi Governor of Bohemia and Moravia, Reinhard Heydrich, this small village was one of several arbitrarily singled out for reprisal. The men were herded into a farmhouse and shot, the women and children were transported to concentration camps and the entire village was razed to the ground. The site is now a shrine with a museum – a wooden cross and a memorial mark the actual place where the men were shot and buried.

✚ 77D2
✉ Information: Smetanovo náměstí 72
☎ (461) 612 161
🕐 Château: May–Aug Tue–Sun 8–12,1–5, Sep 9–12, 1–4, Apr, Oct Sat–Sun 9–12, 1–4
🍴 Café (£), restaurant (££) in town
♿ Few
💷 Cheap
❓ Jun–Jul: Smetana's Litomyšl (opera festival)

LITOMYŠL ✪✪

This attractive town boasts one of the largest squares in the Czech Republic, with a Gothic Town Hall and an impressive array of Rennaisance and baroque houses. 'At the Knights', built in 1540, has a superb sculpted façade: attend an art exhibition here and take a look at the panelled Renaissance ceiling. The château was built in 1568–81 by the Italian architects, Giovanni Battista and Udalrico Aostalli. The exterior is decorated with stunning sgraffiti by Šimon Vlach and the private theatre is one of the oldest in Europe. Litomyšl is also famous as the birthplace of the composer Bedřich Smetana. His apartment in the château is now a museum and music festivals take place in his honour throughout the summer.

www.melnik.cz
✚ 76C3
✉ Turistické Informační st: Náměstí Mírů
☎ (315) 627 503; château: (315) 622 121
🕐 Château: May, Jun, Sep Tue–Sun 9–5, Jul–Aug Tue–Sun 9–6
🍴 Cafés/restaurants (£–£££)
🚌 Bus from Florenc coach station, Prague
♿ None 💷 Moderate

MĚLNÍK ✪✪✪

Perched on a hilltop, with commanding views across the confluence of the Vltava and Labe (Elbe) rivers, is the château, Melnik's main tourist attraction. Founded in the 10th century, it originally belonged to the Bohemian royal family and was occupied by several queens, including the wives of John of Luxemburg and Charles IV, who is credited with introducing wine-making to the region. The castle passed into the hands of the Lobkowicz family early in the 17th century and they have owned it intermittently ever since. Mainly of baroque appearance, its northern wing has an impressive Renaissance arcade and loggia with sgraffito decoration, dating from 1555. The rooms have been refurbished in a variety of styles; most interesting is the Large Bedroom, which contains an early 17th-century canopied bed with a painting of the Madonna at the head. Visitors are also shown trophies and mementos belonging to one of the château's more recent owners, Jiří Christian Lobkowicz, a talented racing driver who died tragically on a track in Berlin in 1932. There is a separate entrance charge for a tour of the remarkable 13th-century wine cellars, with tastings. Mělník's grapes are of the Traminer and Riesling varieties but the climate is not ideal for viniculture – the last good year was 1992.

Mělník Château and the Church of St Peter and Paul are reflected in the placid Labe River

Tours are also available of the Church of St Peter and Paul, built in 1480–1520. Its extended nave is roofed with splendid network and star vaulting and decorated with Renaissance and baroque paintings, including work by Karel Skřeta. The 'pewter' font is actually made of wood. The main draw here is the crypt with its fascinating charnel house, stacked from floor to ceiling with orderly rows of heaped bones – some 15,000 of them at the last count. Some of the skulls are fractured or dented – the result not of careless handling but of bullet wounds sustained in the battles of the Thirty Years' War.

Wine growing is celebrated in Mělník's annual festival

PLZEŇ ✪

www.plzen-city.cz
- 76B2
- Information: náměstí Republiky 41
- Brewery: (19) 706 2755; museum: 224 105
- Brewery: daily 12.30 only unless booked in advance. Pivovarské Muzeum: daily 10–6
- Cafés (£), restaurants (££)
- Praha Hlavní Nádraží
- Few Moderate

Beer has been brewed in Plzeň since 1295 and the Pilsner Urquell brewery is the main attraction in this largely industrial town. The guided tour of the cellars (there are 9km in all) includes a visit to the extravagantly decorated beer hall, definitely an experience not to be missed. Close by is a fascinating Museum of Brewing housed, appropriately enough, in a medieval malthouse. Plzeň's main square, Náměstí Republiky, has some fine Renaissance and baroque town houses and is dominated by the Gothic Cathedral of St Bartholomew, which boasts the tallest steeple in the country (102m).

TÁBOR ✪✪✪

www.tabor.cz
- 76C2
- Infocentrum: Žižkovo náměstí 2
- (3861) 486 230
- Town Hall Museum: Apr–Oct daily 8.30–5, Nov–Mar Mon–Fri 8.30–5
- Cafés (£), restaurants (££)
- Praha hlavní Nádraží
- None Cheap
- Sep: Tabor Meetings, a festival of parades, music, jousting and events

Marvellously situated on a bluff commanding the Lužnice Valley, Tábor takes its name from the Biblical Mountain where Christ is said to have appeared transfigured to his disciples. After the death of Jan Hus, the Hussites transferred their allegiance to the one-eyed general, Jan Žižka, who continued the struggle against the Catholics. He encamped here in 1420 and held out successfuly for four years until his death in battle. The town's attractive main square, about 20 minutes' walk from the station, is called after him and there is a statue by Josef Strachovksý.

The tower of the Church of the Transfiguration, which dates from the 16th century, offers the best views of the gabled Renaissance and classical housés and of the town itself, which is seen melting into the distance.

An exhibition in the neo-Gothic Town Hall presents an excellent account of the Hussite Movement. Don't miss the tour of the labyrinthine tunnels, 600m below ground. Dating from the 15th century, they were used variously as beer cellars, as a prison for unruly women and as an escape route in time of war. When you emerge, you'll find yourself near a café where you can sit and relax. The narrow twisting streets of the Old Town are a delight, although you may get lost from time to time. This is no accident – when the town was laid out Žižka's followers wanted to make life as confusing as possible for the enemy. A pleasant stroll along the banks of the Lužnice River leads to the Bechyň Gate and Kotnov Castle, with its distictive round tower. Inside are some fascinating displays on medieval life in the region, with costumes, archaeological finds, farming implements and weapons. The fabulous views from the tower are a bonus.

Only 2km away, across beautiful countryside, is the hamlet of Klokoty, with a baroque convent and church dating from the early 18th century. The wayside shrines along the footpath mark it out as a place of Catholic pilgrimage.

On the other side of town, between Žižkova and Tržní náměstí, is a Renaissance water tower decorated with vaulted gables and dating from 1497. The water was pumped to the town's seven fountains from the Jordan, the oldest dam in Europe, via a system of wooden pipes.

Above: *the 16th-century Church of the Transfiguration dominates the main square in Tábor*

Opposite: *equestrian statue of the Hussite leader Jan Žižka in Tábor's Town Hall Museum*

www.pamatnik-terezin.cz

- 76B3
- Information: Principova alej 304
- (416) 782 225
- Apr–Oct daily 9–6, Nov–Mar 10–4
- Restaurant (£)
- Coach from Praha Florenc
- None
- Moderate

TEREZÍN ✪

In 1942 the Nazis turned Terezín into a ghetto and transit camp for Jews. More than 150,000 people ended up in extermination camps, while a further 35,000 died of disease and starvation. At the same time the Germans used Terezín for their perverted propaganda purposes, persuading Red Cross visitors that this was a flourishing cultural and commercial centre. The exhibition in the main fortress, now restored after the flood, gives an excellent if harrowing account of the realities of life in the camp, while across the river, in the lesser fortress, visitors can tour the barracks, workshops, isolation cells, mortuaries, execution grounds and former mass graves.

- 76C1
- Information: Masarykovo náměstí 103
- (384) 721 169
- Château: May–Sep Tue–Sun 9–noon, 1–5
- Cafés (£), restaurants (££)
- Praha hlavní Nádraží
- Few
- České Budějovice (➤ 78)

The ponds around Třeboň have been stocked with carp since the 14th century

TŘEBOŇ ✪✪

The charming spa town of Třeboň is best known for the quality of its carp ponds, which date back to the 14th century – Carp Rožmberk is on the menu of many restaurants even today. Four surviving gates lead into the walled Old Town which has at its heart a beautiful, elongated square. Dating from 1566, the Town Hall is decorated with three coats of arms: those of the town and its wealthy patrons, the Rožmberks and the Schwarzenbergs. Opposite is the 16th-century White Horse Inn, which has an unusual turreted gable. Třeboň has its own brewery and horse-drawn drays deliver Regent beer to the local hotels and restaurants. The Augustinian monastery church of St Giles dates from 1367 and contains a number of Gothic features, including a statue of the Madonna. The attractive Renaissance château is open to the public and was built in 1562 by the Rožmberk family.

Where To...

Above: *Staroměstské náměstí café*
Right: *At the Two Cats bar*

Restaurants

Prices
Prices are approximate, based on a three-course meal for one without drinks and service:

£££ = over 1000Kč
££ = 500Kč–1000Kč
£   = under 500Kč

Cover charge
Be aware that most restaurants make an extra cover charge rendering the meal more expensive than at first anticipated.

Ambiente (££)
A colourful Czech-owned restaurant which specialises in American cuisine. The servings of ribs, chicken wings, spinach baked potato and pesto pasta are invariably generous. Booking is advised.
✉ Mánesova 59, Praha 2 ☎ 2227 27851 🚇 Jiřího z Poděbrad

Ariana (£)
Prague isn't usually associated with Afghan cooking but that's what's on offer at this eatery. Spicy kebabs, basmati rice and lashings of yogurt are the order of the day. Good value.
✉ Rámová 6, Praha 1 ☎ 2223 23438 🚇 Náměstí Republiky

Arzenal (£££)
Renowned Czech architect Bořek Šípek's stunning glass shop front and gallery paves the way for a superb Thai restaurant that has attracted numerous celebrity visitors. Good fish, curries and vegetarian dishes.
✉ Valentinská 11, Praha 1 ☎ 2248 14099 🚇 Staroměstská

Buffalo Bills (££)
A Tex-Mex eaterie offering the usual *fajitas, tacos, quesadillas* etc. Informal atmosphere with country music.
✉ Vodičkova 9, Praha 1 ☎ 2249 48624 🚇 Můstek 🚌 3, 9, 14, 24, 52, 53, 55, 56

Byblos (£££)
Expensive atmospheric Lebanese restaurant.Try opting for the fixed-price Byblos mezze menu for two, with Middle Eastern dishes like *tabbouleh* and Lebanese sausages. International menu also available.
✉ Rybná 14, Praha 1 ☎ 2218 42121 🚇 Náměstí Republiky

Café Louvre (£)
Franz Kafka used to discuss philosophy here in the early 1900s. The upstairs restaurant is a friendly, no-frills eating house that keeps pool tables in the back room. Serves breakfast.
✉ Národní třída 20, Praha 1 ☎ 2249 30949 🚇 Národní třída 🚌 6, 9, 18, 22, 51

Caffè-Ristorante Italia (££)
Traditional Italian specialities are served in this bright, modern restaurant on one of the loveliest streets in Prague, not far away from the castle.
✉ Nerudova 17 ☎ 2575 32818 🚌 22

Celebrity Café (££)
Much favoured by locals and largely undiscovered by tourists. Light but refined meals – everything from pasta to steaks and traditional Czech fare, is given the *nouvelle cuisine* treatment.
✉ Vinohradská 40, Praha 2 ☎ 2225 11343 🚇 Náměstí Míru

Chez Marcel (££)
A pleasant, modern restaurant serving simple but excellent French country fare, for example, quiches, grilled rabbit in mustard and French mussels.
✉ Haštalská 12, Praha 1 ☎ 2223 15676 🚇 Náměstí Republiky 🚌 5, 14, 26

Clementinum (££)
Cool, predominantly white décor and relaxed ambience is a hit with locals and tourists alike. The dishes can

be described as international with a French twist.

✉ **Platnéřská 9, Praha 1** ☎ **2248 13892** Ⓜ **Staroměstská**

David (£££)

Rather formal, attractively situated restaurant in the Malá Strana. Mainly meat dishes with a continental flavour. Reserve ahead.

✉ **Tržiště 21, Praha 1** ☎ **2575 33109** Ⓜ **Malostranské** 🚊 **12, 27, 57**

Don Giovanni (££)

A welcoming trattoria, only a stone's throw from the Vltava. The *scaloppina di vitello* is recommended. The owner is proud of his more than 30 varieties of home-made grappa.

✉ **Karolíny světlé 34, Praha 1** ☎ **2222 22060** Ⓜ **Narodní Trida** 🚊 **17, 18, 51, 54**

Dynamo (££)

A useful spot for lunch in a back street location not far from the National Theatre. The menu includes potato wedges, spicy chicken, peppered steak with corn on the cob and tagliatelle.

✉ **Pštrossova 29, Praha 1** ☎ **2249 3202** Ⓜ **Národní třída**

Grossetto (£)

Judging by the queues, this must be Prague's most popular pizza-pasta restaurant of the moment. The secret of its success probably lies in the uniformly generous helpings.

✉ **Francouzská 2, Praha 2** ☎ **2242 52778** Ⓜ **Náměstí Míru**

Hanavsky Pavilon (£££)

An iron constructed neo-baroque pavilion in Letná Park. Diners are attracted by the expensive but delicious international and Czech dishes.

✉ **Letenské sady 173, Praha 6** ☎ **2333 23641** Ⓜ **Malostranská** 🚊 **12**

Haveli (£££)

Not many Indian restaurants can boast this beautiful cellar setting. Good, if expensive regional dishes, including a respectable number of vegetarian offerings.

✉ **Dejvická 6, Praha 6** ☎ **2333 44800** Ⓜ **Hradčanská**

Hlučna Samota (££)

A traditional Czech restaurant with an English menu that is strong on fish as well as meat dishes and, while the portions are predictably substantial, the sprightly vegetable accompaniment is a refreshing change.

✉ **Záhřebská 14, Praha 2** ☎ **2225 22839** Ⓜ **Náměstí Míru**

Huang He (£)

While Prague isn't exactly renowned for its Chinese restaurants, this one bucks the trend and is worth tracking down. No frills but an excellent range of fish and meat dishes nonetheless, and at bargain prices.

✉ **Vršovická 1 Praha 10** ☎ **2717 46651** 🚊 **tram 7, 24 to nádraží Vršovice**

Kampa Park (£££)

A wonderful location on Kampa Island, overlooking the Vltava. Softly lit ambience and delightful specialities, including fresh lobster and game. Bookings essential for the terrace.

✉ **Na Kampě 8b, Praha 1** ☎ **2575 32685** Ⓜ **Malostranská** 🚊 **Tram 22 to Malostranské náměstí**

The Nut Trick

When eating out in Prague expect to pay for everything – few restaurateurs are in the habit of offering a free aperitif or a liqueur. Even the nibbles carry a price tag, as you may discover to your cost when the bill arrives and you are charged more for the nuts than for the appetiser. The best advice is send them back before you order and always say no unless you are a personal friend of the manager!

Culinary Delights

Eating out has never been more enjoyable in Prague. No longer do visitors have to queue outside for a table or suffer slow, surly service and meals high on quantity but low on everything else. Prague is also becoming more international in its culinary habits. Italian trattorias and pizzerias currently lead the field, but hot on the trail are the Americans, the French, the Japanese, the Yugoslavs and the Lebanese.

Kolkovna (£–££)

A lively pub restaurant with an eye-catching art nouveau interior. The hearty Czech pub grub creates few surprises but will leave no stomach unfilled. Good beer.

🖂 **V Kolkovně 8, Praha 1**
☎ **2248 19701**
🚇 **Staroměstská**

La Provence (£££)

Robert Chejn, the chef at this very popular (and therefore very busy) French restaurant, presents the usual Gallic specialities, from cassoulet to coq au vin. Attentive service but some of the waiters are over-anxious about tips.

🖂 **Štupartská 9, Praha 1**
☎ **2575 35050** 🚇 **Náměstí Republiky**

La Perle de Prague (£££)

Located in the arresting Tančici dům (one of the finer examples of modern architecture), this French restaurant has unbeatable views of the Vltava.

🖂 **Rašinovo nábřeží 80, Praha 2, by Jiráskův bridge**
☎ **2219 84160** 🚇 **Karlovo náměstí** 🚌 **3, 17, 21**

La Veranda (£££)

With a former 'chef of the year' in the kitchen, a superb meal is only to be expected. Radek David's creative way with fusion cooking continues to win him admirers. Pricey but definitely worth it.

🖂 **Elišky Krásnohorské 2, Praha 10** ☎ **2248 14733**
🚇 **Staroměstská**

Le Bistro de Marlène (£££)

A little out of the way unless you happen to be visiting Vyšehrad, this excellent French restaurant is run by highly resourceful owner/chef Marlène Salomon.

🖂 **Plavecká 4, Praha 2**
☎ **2249 21853** 🚌 **7, 18, 24**

Miyabi (££)

Miyabi is owned by a Czech who lived in Japan for many years. The menu is a deliciously ingenious mixture of home-grown Czech ingredients cooked in a Japanese style.

🖂 **Navratilova 10, Praha 1**
☎ **2962 33102** 🚇 **Karlovo náměstí** 🚌 **3, 9, 14, 24, 52, 53**

Nagoya (££)

Japanese cuisine has taken Central Europe by storm in recent years and once you've visited this fine restaurant you'll appreciate why. True, the menu of (predominantly) sushi, sashimi and tempura dishes offers few surprises but there are no duds either.

🖂 **Stroupežnického 23, Praha 5**
☎ **2515 11724** 🚇 **Anděl**

Obecní dům (£–£££)

There are several dining spaces in this wonderful art nouveau monument. The most formal is the so-called French restaurant (the cuisine is international). Downstairs there's the Plzenská Czech Restaurant, designed like a beer keller; while the café on the ground floor serves pancakes and other snacks (▶ 61).

🖂 **Náměstí Republiky 5, Praha 1** ☎ **2220 02101** 🚇 **Náměstí Republiky**

Olympos (££)

Popular low-price Greek eatery restaurant serving the usual national delicacies. Outdoor dining is possible, either in the courtyard or the winter garden.

✉ **Kubelikova 9, Praha 1** ☎ **2227 22239** 🚇 **Jiřiho z Poděbrad**

Pálffy Palác (£££)

Dine out in the baroque surroundings of this sumptuous 17th-century palace beneath Prague Castle. Great food too. Reservations advisable.

✉ **Valdštejnská 14, Praha 1**
☎ **2575 30522**
🚇 **Malostranská** 🚋 **22**

Pizzeria Kmotra (££)

So popular that queues often stretch into the street, this excellent restaurant offers a wide range of pizza fillings.

✉ **Vjirchářích 12, Praha 1**
☎ **2249 34100** 🚇 **Národní třída** 🚋 **6, 9, 18, 22, 51**

Pizzeria Rugantino (££)

A good lunchtime stopover for visitors to Josefov: the pizzas here are satisfying.

✉ **Dušní 4, Praha 1** ☎ **2223 18172** 🚋 **17**

Red Hot and Blues (££)

A lively Cajun/Tex-Mex restaurant that serves tasty shrimp gumbo, bean burritos and the usual range of burgers. Brunch served until 4PM, Sat and Sun.

✉ **Jakubská 12, Praha 1**
☎ **2223 14639** 🚇 **Náměstí Republiky** 🚋 **5, 14, 26**

Reykjavik (££)

Fish soup and salmon are among the dishes on offer in this stylish restaurant. Efficient, friendly service.

✉ **Karlova 20, Praha 1**
☎ **2222 21218**
🚇 **Staroměstská** 🚋 **17, 18, 51**

Rudý Baron (££)

The eye-catching décor of 'The Red Baron' pays tribute to the famous First World War flying ace. The mainly meaty fare is nothing special but the children will love it - if less than 120cm tall they dine free.

✉ **Korunny 23, Praha 2**
☎ **2225 11348** 🚇 **Náměstí Míru**

Rybí trh (£££)

'The Fish Market' has a nice location in the courtyard behind the Týn Church. Its reputation for quality freshwater and sea fish and shellfish, served stewed, grilled or roasted according to taste, is thoroughly deserved, so expect to pay for the privilege.

✉ **Týnský Dvůr 5, Praha 1**
☎ **2248 95447**
🚇 **Staroměstská**

Saté Grill (£)

A small, unpretentious Indonesian restaurant, which serves cheap, spicy chicken and meat dishes – handy for lunch after sightseeing.

✉ **Pohořelec 3, Praha 1**
☎ **2205 14552** 🚋 **22**

Seven Angels (££)

You'll be in seventh heaven when you dine in the simple Gothic surroundings of this 13th century dining space. The menu offers the usual Czech fare – roasts, dumplings, potato pancakes and the like.

✉ **Jilská 20, Praha 1** ☎ **2242 34381** 🚇 **Můstek**

Taj Mahal (££)

The décor is nothing to write home about but the Indian food, mainly standards like chicken *tikka masala*, is excellent and authentic.

✉ **Škretova 10, Praha 2**
☎ **2242 25666** 🚇 **Muzeum**

Late Breakfast

One consequence of the post-1989 American invasion of Prague has been the increasing availability of Sunday brunch. Options range from the vegetarian menu at Radost FX (► 97) to the traditional ham and eggs at Molly Malone's. For a touch of spice try Red Hot and Blues (► 95), which serves up *huevos rancheros*, Mexican-style. Or, if the money is burning a hole in your wallet, there is always the buffet at V Zátiši (► 96), with its large selection of cold cuts, salads and omelettes made to order.

Dumplings

Bohemian dumplings (*knedlíky*) are made from bread, potato dough, soft curd or flour. Necessary accompaniments to meat dishes to soak up the grease and beer, they also come in more sophisticated guises, the best-known being fruit dumplings. The most mouth-watering versions are filled with plums, strawberries, sour cherries or apricots, with a topping of melted butter and icing sugar – not good for the waistline!

U bílé kravy (££–£££)

The tongue-in-cheek farmhouse décor includes grazing white cattle, appropriately as the speciality here is prime cuts of Charolais beef, beautifully prepared and served. Moravian as well as Burgundy wines are available by way of accompaniment. Closed Sat, Sun.

✉ **Rubešova 10, Praha 2**
☎ **2242 39570** 🚇 **IP Pavlova**

U Kalicha (£££)

Immortalised in Jaroslav Hašek's novel *The Good Soldier Schweik* (you can see the green-uniformed hero on the sign outside), this restaurant is specially popular with tourists and serves traditional Czech fare.

✉ **Na Bojišti 12-14, Praha 2**
☎ **2249 16475** 🚇 **IP Pavlova**
🚋 **4, 6, 15, 16, 22**

U Maltézských Rytířů (££)

An attractively sedate restaurant in the Malá Strana. Delicious Czech cuisine with the emphasis on game, although salmon and other fish are also on the menu. Book ahead for a table in the Gothic cellar.

✉ **Prokopská 10, Praha 1**
☎ **2575 33666** 🚋 **12, 27, 57**

U Mecenáše (£££)

Fresh game dishes are served in this luxurious establishment with vaulted ceilings and medieval beams.

✉ **Malostranské náměstí 10, Praha 1** ☎ **2575 31631**
🚇 **Malostranská** 🚋 **12, 27, 57**

U Modré Růže (£££)

Such exotic dishes as turtle soup, ostrich and alligator are served in an elegant 15th-century wine cellar. There is an additional 50Kčs per person cover charge for the pianist.

✉ **Rytiýská 16, Praha 1**
☎ **2242 25873** 🚇 **Můstek**

U tří housliček (££)

'At the Three Fiddles' dates from the 16th century and was once owned by a violin maker. There are set menu options drawing from the à la carte list of fish and game specialities.

✉ **Nerudova 12, Praha 1**
☎ **2575 32062** 🚋 **22**

U Vladaře (£££)

Attractively located in Maltese Square, this expensive but high quality restaurant specialises in old Prague favourites – such dishes as leg of boar in garlic and juniper berries, for instance, and roast goose with cabbage and three kinds of dumplings!

✉ **Maltézské náměstí 10, Praha 1** ☎ **2575 34121** 🚋 **12, 27, 57**

U Zlaté hrušky (£££)

'At the Golden Pear' enjoys a romantic location in a lane behind Prague Castle. Beautifully prepared international dishes with a French accent.

✉ **Nový Svět 3, Praha 1**
☎ **2205 14778** 🚋 **22**

V Zátiší (££)

One of relatively few restaurants to cater for vegetarians, V Zátiší attracts a loyal clientele, drawn to the food as well as to the intimate surroundings. Set menus are offered, as well as à la carte.

✉ **Liliová 1, Praha 1** ☎ **2222 21155** 🚋 **17, 18, 51, 54**

Cafés

Bohemia Bagel (£)
A friendly self-service café where you can eat freshly-baked bagels until they come out of your ears. They also do regular sandwiches, quiches, brownies and cookies.
✉ Újezd 16, Praha 1 ☎ 2573 10694 🚇 Malostranská 🚋 12, 22

Café de Paris (££)
Admire the arresting art nouveau interior of this sedate hotel café. There is excellent jazz served up on Thursdays and Gateau Paříževery day.
✉ U Obecního domu 1, Praha 1 ☎ 2242 22151 🚇 Náměstí Republiky

Caffé Ledebour (££)
Although the food is not particularly remarkable, the most attractive thing about this café is the setting. It is housed in an old palace coaching house with a glorious painted baroque ceiling.
✉ Valdštejnské náměstí 3, Praha 1 ☎ 2570 10412 🚇 Malostranská

Country Life (£)
Central self-service vegetarian restaurant where all the dishes use only plant based ingredients.
✉ Melantrichova 15, Praha 1 ☎ 2421 3366 🚇 Můstek

Kaaba (£)
A relative newcomer to the Prague café scene, Kaaba is a great place to rest from sightseeing. They sell coffees from all over the world; good Czech wines, too.
✉ Mánesova 20, Praha 2 ☎ 2222 54021 🚇 Jiřiho z Poděbrad

Káva, Káva, Káva (£)
As the name suggests, it's coffee galore in this rambling busy café. They also serve sandwiches, light lunches and cocktails and there are Internet facilities too.
✉ Národní 37, Praha 1, ☎ 2242 28862 🚇 Národní třída

Kavárna ve Šternberskén Palči (£)
A haven for non-smokers, this café situated in the Šternberg Palace serves salads and snacks at very reasonable prices. Open only during gallery hours.
✉ Hradčanské náměstí 15, Praha 1 ☎ (gallery) 2248 10758 🚋 22

Radost FX Café (££)
A favourite with ex-patriates, the 'Fun' café is not really the place to come to meet locals. The all-vegetarian menu is a definite draw for its novelty. Weekend brunch available.
✉ Bělehradská 120, Praha 2 ☎ 2242 54776 🚋 6, 11

Restaurant Jarmark (£)
Amazingly cheap self-service restaurant in the Lucerna Passage. There are appetising salads, grills, stir-fries, pastries, fresh fruit and more. No one ever leaves hungry!
✉ Vodičkova 30, Praha 1 ☎ 2242 33733 🚋 3, 9, 14, 24

The Globe Bookstore and Coffeehouse (£)
This café offers a mix of coffee, English conversation and tempting American-style desserts such as brownies and muffins.
✉ Pštrosova 6, Praha 1 ☎ 2249 34203 🚇 Národní třída 🚋 6, 9, 17, 21, 22, 23, 51

Time for Tea
Like Vienna, Prague is traditionally more associated with coffee houses than with tea rooms, but the latter are proving increasingly popular, especially with visitors. Two to try: Dobrá čajovna, ✉ Václavské náměstí 14, and U Zeleného čaje, ✉ Nerudova 19, which serves vegetarian pizzas, salads and tofu and sells teapots, mugs, honey, joss sticks and other accessories.

Restaurants Outside Prague

Spirit of the Times?
Following a court ruling in favour of the German firm of Underberg, Becherovka, the famous liqueur associated with Karlovy Vary since it was invented in 1807, will be produced in Germany as well as the Czech Republic. The dispute cost the Karlovarská Becherovska distillery an estimated 40 per cent of the German export market and Underberg acquired a significant holding in the firm following privitisation.

Brno

Zahradní Restaurace (££)
The 'Garden Restaurant' has long been celebrated for its Chinese cuisine, but the Moravian dishes, heavily laced with paprika, are also worth trying. Pleasant ambience and very reasonable prices.
✉ **Grandhotel Brno, Benešova 18–20** ☎ **(5) 4232 1287**

České Budějovice

Malý Pivovar (££)
A delightful café and restaurant in the historic premises of the 'small brewery', where beer has been on sale since 1722.
✉ **Karla IV 8/95**
☎ **(386) 360 471**

U Hrušků (££)
Just round the corner from the Town Hall, 'At the Pear' serves a wide range of meals and drinks. It also caters happily for tour groups.
✉ **Česká 23**
☎ **(38) 731 8099**

Česky Krumlov

Krčma Markéta (££)
A period Renaissance pub within the château gardens, where chicken and game are served after being cooked over an open fire. Drinks are presented in pewter mugs and 'servants' appear wearing medieval costumes. Music is also performed.
✉ **Latrán 37**
☎ **(380) 711 487**

Pivnice Eggenberg (££)
A beer bar and restaurant in the historic Eggenberg

brewery. Czech specialities are served here, and, needless to say, there is also plenty of excellent beer – light and dark – on tap.
✉ **Latrán 27**
☎ **(380) 711 426**

Restaurant Jelenka (££)
Period restaurant serving traditional Bohemian cuisine. Meals can be enjoyed on the large terrace.
✉ **Latrán 138**
☎ **(380) 711 283**

Karlovy Vary

Pizzeria Palermo (£)
Aficionados of the pizza–pasta combination rate this the best in town for food and atmosphere.
✉ **Moskevská 44**
☎ **(353) 234 222**

Promenáda (£££)
A hit with the locals, this much sought-after dining spot serves Czech specialities, international cuisine and vegetarian dishes. There is also a selection of more than 70 wines dating back to 1974. Advance reservations are recommended.
✉ **Tržiště 31**
☎ **(353) 225 648**

Kutná Hora

Piazza Navona (££)
A busy Italian restaurant and pizzeria with terrace tables, just off the main square. Multi-lingual menu. Takes all credit and debit cards.
✉ **Palackého náměsti 90**
☎ **(327) 512 588**

U Havířů (££)
Czech *vinarna* (wine cellar), where there is dancing as

well as eating and drinking. Medieval feasts arranged for parties.

✉ Šultysova 154
☎ (327) 513 997

U Morového Sloupu (££)
Small intimate restaurant with a pleasing garden terrace. Takes all cards.

✉ Šultysova 173
☎ (327) 513 810

Mělník

U Cinků (££)
Garden restaurant offering Czech and Italian specialities, as well as a selection of fish dishes.

✉ Českolipská 1166
☎ (206) 670401

Vinárna U Tomáše (£)
A relaxed and friendly local restaurant that offers a varied Czech menu and local wines.

✉ Náměstí Miru 30
☎ (206) 627357

Plzeň

Na stilce (£££)
A large beer hall on the premises of the Prazdroj (Pilsner Urquell) Brewery; serving a range of Czech and international dishes – although most customers are here for the beer.

✉ Veleslavínova 6
☎ (19) 706 2755

U Salzmannů (££)
The oldest pub in town, serves Czech and international cuisine in simple but attractive surroundings with beer, naturally enough, available on tap.

✉ Pražská 8
☎ (19) 723 5855

Tábor

Atrium (££)
Located in the atrium of the new Slovan Commercial Centre, this Czech restaurant also serves a selection of Moravian wines.

✉ Slovan Centre, 9 Května
☎ (381) 498 307

U Červeného Koně (££)
If you're not put off by horse(!) on the menu – hence the name 'At the Red Horse', you'll enjoy the more conventional Czech dishes.

✉ Křizíkova 31
☎ (381) 255 320

U Kalicha (££)
In the historic centre of Tábor, this traditional restaurant serves Czech and international dishes.

✉ Žizkovo náměstí
☎ (381) 251 927

Třeboň

Bistro U Kapra (£)
Třeboň is famous for its carp ponds and this is as good a place as any to sample the area's fish specialities. Meat dishes also available.

✉ Dukelská 106
☎ (602) 272 829

Šupina Bar-Restaurant (££)
Fish specialities are served inside the restaurant, as well as on the terrace.

✉ Valy 155
☎ (384) 721 149

U Čochtana (££)
Housed in historic surroundings, this wine cellar dates from the 18th century. Excellent Czech cuisine is served here.

✉ Březanova 7
☎ (384) 724 740

Czech Beer
Beer has been brewed in Plžeň since the town was founded in 1295 but the Prazdrój Bresery (Pilsner Urquell) dates from 1842. Visitors to the museum, located in a Gothic malthouse, learn all about brewing technology and have a chance to see the historic lager cellars. Beer-tasting is also part of the package, and meals are served in the Na spilce restaurant.

Prague

Prices

Prices are approximate, per room per night.

£££ = over 3,000Kč
££ = 1,500–3,000Kč
£ = under1,500Kč

Europa Hotel

Originally known as the 'Archduke Stepan', the Europa Hotel was rebuilt in 1903–5 by two leading exponents of art nouveau architecture, Bedřich Bendelamayer and Alois Dryák. The façade, overlooking Wenceslas Square, is decorated with graceful sculpted figures, elaborate wrought-iron balconies and a gable with a mosaic of coloured glass by Jan Förster. The decoration of the restaurant is even more extraordinary; particularly beautiful are the bronze lamps, supported by angels with flowing robes.

Betlem Club (££)

The name is a give away – this small hotel is situated just across the street from the Bethlehem Chapel, where the reformer Jan Hus preached in the 15th century. Easy access to the Old Town and there are bars and restaurants on the square.

Betlémské náměstí 9, Praha 1 ☎ 2222 21575; www.betlemclub.cz
Národní třída

Bílý Lev (££)

The location of the 'White Lion' in the eastern suburb of Žižkov may be a little remote, but prices and facilities are reasonable.

Cimburkova 20, Praha 3 ☎ 2227 8043 5, 9, 26

Černy slon (£££)

A tastefully reconstructed, UNESCO-protected 14th century house, only a stone's throw from Old Town Square. Rooms are spacious and furnished with antiques. No lift.

Týnská 629/1, Praha 1 ☎ 2223 21521; www.hotelcernyslon.cz
Náměstí Republiky

Corinthia Towers Hotel (£££)

This modern high-rise is fairly remote from the centre but is accessible by metro. What you pay for are the comprehensive facilities, including restaurants, shops, bars, a fitness centre and bowling alley.

Kongresová 1, Praha 4 ☎ 2611 91111; www.corinthia.cz
Vyšehrad

Elysee (££)

Newly built hotel with a convenient location overlooking Wencelas Square. All 70 rooms are of generous size and some are adapted for visitors with disabilities.

Václavské náměstí 43, Praha 1 ☎ 2242 25772; www.europehotels.cz
Vyšehrad

Estec Hostel Strahov (£)

Reasonable access to Prague Castle is one of this hostel's advantages. Facilities include a breakfast room and bar. If Estec is booked up try the Petros and Sakbuild hostels up the road.

Vaničkova 5/ blok 5, Praha 6 ☎ 2572 10410; www.estec.cz
Dejvická

Hotel Adria (£££)

This completely renovated hotel near the Franciscan Gardens has excellent facilities, including satellite TV, bars, fitness centre, choice of restaurants etc.

Václavské náměstí 26, Praha 1 ☎ 2210 81111
Můstek

Hotel Bílá Labut (££)

The reasonably priced 'White Swan' boasts an excellent location on the edge of the Old Town. Satellite TV and there is a night bar and restaurant.

Biskupská 9, Praha 1 ☎ 2248 11382 Florenc

Hotel Hoffmeister (£££)

Prague's beautifully refurbished 'personal luxury hotel' enjoys an enviable position below the bend on the road leading up to Prague Castle.

Pod bruskou 7, Praha 1 ☎ 2510 17111; www.hoffmeister.cz
Malostranská

Hotel Nusle-Garni (££)
Good value modern hotel at the Vyšehrad end of town. Bar snacks available all day.
✉ Závišova 30, Praha 4
☎ 2215 98165 🚊 7, 18, 24

Hotel Paříž (£££)
An eye-catching neo-Gothic building with art nouveau flourishes, the Paříž has undergone extensive restoration work and is now considered to be one of the city's top hotels.
✉ U Obecního domu 1, Praha 1
☎ 2221 95195 🚇 Náměstí Republiky

Hotel Pension City (£)
A real bargain. Only one metro stop from Wenceslas Square, the rooms in this spotless and well-run pension are airy and spacious. Good buffet breakfast included in the price.
✉ Belgická 10, Praha 2
☎ 2225 21606 🚇 Náměstí Míru

Pension Páv (££)
Comfortable hotel located in historical old Prague. Proximity to the famous brewery, U Fleků means some rooms can be very noisy in the early evening.
✉ Křemencova 13, Praha 1
☎ 2249 33760; www.pension-pav.cz 🚇 Národní třída

Romantik Hotel U Raka (£)
Situated in the picturesque Nový Svět, this small pension is in great demand, so book well in advance.
✉ Černínská 10, Praha 1
☎ 2205 11100 🚊 22

Savoy (£££)
One of Prague's leading hotels, the Savoy is only a stone's throw from Hradčany. The rooms are well appointed and there's a reassuringly unhurried ambience.
✉ Kapelerova 6, Praha 1
☎ 2243 02430 🚊 22

U Krále Jiřího (£)
A popular pension located above two Old Town bars, this is inevitably noisy at night unless you can get one of the back rooms. All rooms are equipped with showers, telephones and televisions and there's a bar and restaurant.
✉ Liliová 10, Praha 1
☎ 2242 48797
🚇 Staroměstská

U Tří Pštrosů (£££)
Once the centre of a flourishing trade in feathers (▶ panel), 'At the Three Ostriches' is a charming hostelry with a good location near the Charles Bridge. The restaurant has a deservedly good reputation offering some excellent fish dishes.
✉ Dražického náměstí 12, Praha 1 ☎ 2575 32410
🚇 Malostranská

Villa Voyta (££)
A charming suburban hotel, designed as a roadside inn in 1912 by art nouveau architect, Josef Vojtěch. Excellent French restaurant with regularly changing menu.
✉ K Novému dvoru 124/54, Praha 4 ☎ 2617 11307

Accommodation Agencies

Prague Bed and Breakfast Association
This well-established agency offers private and hotel accommodation in all price categories. The helpful staff speak English.
✉ Kroftova 3, Praha 5
☎ 2573 26897 🚊 6, 9, 12

PIS (Prague Information Service)
The accommodation on offer from the Prague Information Service is mainly in pensions or private homes.
✉ Na Příkopě 20, Praha 1
☎ 2242 26087 🚇 Můstek

The Three Ostriches
One of Prague's most charming hotels is the quaintly named 'At the Three Ostriches' (U Tří Pštrosů). It was built in 1606 by Jan Fux, a well-known supplier of ostrich feathers to the nobility, who used them to decorate their caps and hats. The restored interiors have preserved the original painted wooden Renaissance ceilings, together with some of the antique furniture.

Outside Prague

Finding a Room in Brno

Visitors to Brno should be aware that the demand for accommodation during Trade Fairs is high and that some hotels are frequently booked out. (Price hikes can also be expected.) If you arrive without a place to stay, your best bet is the information office at Radnícká 8, ☎ (542) 211 090.

Brno

Grandhotel Brno (£££)

Brno's best hotel has a prime site opposite the busy railway station. The extensive modern facilities include a nightclub, a casino and two first-class restaurants.

✉ Benešova 18–20 ☎ (542) 518 111; www.grandhotelbrno.cz

České Budějovice

Hotel U Solné Brány (££)

An attractive hotel in the quiet location of the Diocesan Gardens. Every room has a balcony and TV and there's a good restaurant.

✉ Radniční ulice 11 ☎ (38) 635 4121

Hotel U Tří Lvů (££)

Located only a few minutes' walk from the main square, 'At the Three Lions' has facilities including its own restaurant, night club and fitness centre.

✉ U Tří Lvů 3a ☎ (38) 635 9000; www.hotelutrilvu.cz

Hotel Grand Zvon (££)

Situated in the town's main square, this large, well-established hotel has been completely renovated and boasts no fewer than three restaurants.

✉ Náměstí Přemysla Otakara II 28 ☎ (38) 7311 3834

Český Krumlov

Hotel Gold (£££)

A modern, attractive hotel with restaurant and wine bar. Horse-riding can be arranged locally for guests.

✉ Plešivec 55, Městsky park ☎ (337) 712 552

Hotel Růže (££)

This stunning Renaissance building overlooking the Vltava dates from 1586–90 and once served as a hostel for members of the Jesuit Order. There are 53 rooms available, including 34 doubles and 12 Jesuit cells (double rooms without facilities for those on retreat). The hotel also has its own café and restaurant and organises sightseeing tours.

✉ Horní 154 ☎ (337) 772 100; www.hotelruze.cz

Pension Falko (£)

All rooms in this modest hotel have shower, WC and minibar and some have satellite TV. Wheelchair access.

✉ Rooseveltova 152 ☎ (337) 716 262

Pension Na Louži (£)

Clean and centrally located pension with its original 1930s interior. Czech restaurant and beer from the barrel

✉ Kájovská 66 ☎ (337) 711 280

Karlovy Vary

Bristol Hotel Palace (£££)

A top-notch spa hotel, with an attractive central location, set in its own grounds. Classical spa therapy is available; as well as several varieties of alternative treatment, including oxygen therapy, lymphatic drainage and an anti-sclerosis programme.

✉ Sadová 19 ☎ (234) 125 229

Dvořák (£££)

The facilities in this top-class hotel are unrivalled, and include such luxuries as a

spa treatment centre, sauna, gym and swimming pool.

✉ **Nová louka 11**
☎ **(234) 125 229**

Hotel Café Elefant (££)

Spa treatment is available at this elegant, but attractively priced hotel off the Market Colonnade. All 17 double rooms (only one single) are fully equiped and there is a pleasant café .

✉ **Stará Louka 30** ☎ **(353) 222 544**

Kutná Hora

Hotel Lorec (£)

There are 45 beds in this clean, modern hotel which also has its own restaurant. Food available all day.

✉ **Lorecká 57** ☎ **(327) 524 455**

Hotel U Růže (£)

A small hotel which has 26 beds available and its own restaurant.

✉ **Zámecká 52** ☎ **(327) 524 115**

Hotel U Vlašského Dvora (££)

A small hotel with good facilities including an exchange office, bar, sauna and satellite TV.

✉ **28 října 511** ☎ **(327) 514 618**

Plzeň

Hotel Slovan (££)

A large, clean, moderately priced hotel with restaurant, café and bar.

✉ **Smetanovy sady 1** ☎ **(19) 722 7256**

Tabor

Hotel Kapital (££)

Twenty-four well-appointed rooms with telephones and TV. The excellent restaurant offers Bohemian and international cuisine and is well recommended.

✉ **9 Května 617** ☎ **(381) 256 096; www.hotel-kapital.cz**

Hotel Palcát (££)

Sixty-eight all-inclusive rooms in this large, modern hotel that also accomodates a bar, restaurant and nightclub.

✉ **9 Května 2471**
☎ **(381) 252 901**

Hotel Relax U Drsů (££)

A large, well-appointed and modern hotel with a wine bar and cellar restaurant, fitness suite, sauna, solarium and aerobics room.

✉ **Varšavská 2708** ☎ **(381) 263 906; www.hotel-relax.cz**

Třeboň

Bílý Koníček (££)

Located in an attractive, castellated building that dates back to the Renaissance period, 'The White Horse' has simply decorated, clean rooms, a restaurant and terrace.

✉ **Masarykovo náměstí 97**
☎ **(384) 721 213**

Pension Siesta (£)

A pleasant, centrally located guest house with clean rooms, an attractive terrace and charming hosts.

✉ **Hradební 26** ☎ **(384) 232 496**

Zlatá Hvědza (££)

Comfortable rooms with an excellent location on the main square. Brewery tours, permits for fishing, horse-riding and cycle hire can all be arranged for guests.

✉ **Masarykovo náměstí 107**
☎ **(333) 757 111**

Private Accommodation

Staying in private accommodation is becoming an increasingly attractive option for visitors to Prague (and elsewhere in the Czech Republic). There are several agencies in the town centre and one or two have branches at the main railway station. Many apartments are in good central locations and, if you come out of season, prices are especially competitive – less than half what you might expect to pay in a hotel. Summer visitors should be sure to book in advance.

Souvenirs

Ideas for Gifts

Prague is most famous for Bohemia Crystal, and it's surprising how reasonable the prices can be. Wooden toys and puppets are not only popular with children but make nice ornaments for teenage bedrooms and around the home. On Old Town Square you'll be able to pick up jester's hats, logo T-shirts and trinkets. You will find Kafka memorabilia all over the place, but the best selection is at the exhibition in U Radnice (➤ 39).

Botanicus

Everything on sale here has come from an organic farm 30km outside Prague. Spices, herbal remedies, candles, toiletries, syrup, honey, shampoos etc.

✉ Týnský Dvůr 3, Praha 1
☎ 2248 95446
🚇 Staroměstská

Celetná Crystal

A large store selling a wide range of garnets, amber, porcelain and Bohemain crystal.

✉ Celetná 15, Praha 1
☎ 2223 24022 🚇 Náměstí Republiky

Ceská lidová remesla

Czech folk art from easter eggs to straw nativities. Branches at Melantrichova, Mostecká and Nerudova.

✉ Železná 3a, Praha 1 ☎ 2222 20403 🚇 Můstek

Crystalland

A huge modern emporium selling a wide range of Czech glassware, crystal and porcelain.

✉ Národní 15, Praha 1
☎ 2242 15265 🚇 Národní třída

Havelské tržiště

This central fruit and vegetable market also has some souvenir and craft stalls.

✉ Havelská, Praha 1
🚇 Můstek

Manufaktura

Huge handicraft shop, stocking everything from crib figures to spoons, also mobiles, basket-ware, handmade soap and glassware.

✉ Karlova 26, Praha 1 ☎ 2216 32480 🚇 Staroměstská

Moser

A selection of superb quality porcelain and crystal for those for whom money is no object. Crystal and porcelain made in Carlsbad (Karlov Vary) and also porcelain from Meissen and Herend.

✉ Na příkopě 12, Praha 1
☎ 2242 11293 🚇 Můstek

Museum Shop Pražský Hrad

Located close to Golden Lane, the shop sells posters, cards, art books, silk ties and scarves, jewellery, glass and porcelain – much of it inspired by Prague's major monuments.

✉ Purkrabství Jiřská ulice 6, Praha 1 ☎ 2243 73368 🚌 22

Old Town Square Market

Souvenirs are on sale here daily, including scarves, wooden toys and wrought-iron work made in the forge.

✉ Staroměstské náměstí, Praha 1 ☎ None
🚇 Staroměstská

Regena

Very convenient for visitors to the Charles Bridge, the shop's large stock of crystalware includes exquisite stained glass, painted glass, high enamel and glass souvenirs.

✉ Karlova 44, Praha 1 ☎ 2242 20560 🚇 Staroměstská

Sklo Bohemia

Sklo Bohemia sells Czech crystal direct from Svá nad Sázavou in the Moravian highlands. This outlet stocks a variety of designs, which include frosted vases, coloured wine glasses and even crystal beer mugs.

✉ Na příkopě 17, Praha 1
☎ 2242 11699 🚇 Můstek

Art & Antiques

Bazar Klipy Antik
A real pot-pourri of the rare and the commonplace, from stamp collections and worn leather jackets to Biedermeier and Louis XVIII furniture.
✉ **Vyšehradská 8, Praha 2**
☎ **2249 12766** 🚋 **18, 24**

Galerie Art Praha
A representative selection of some of the finest contemporary works by Czech artists, including distinguished names like Bohumír Dvorsky and Karel Souček.
✉ **Staroměstské náměstí 20, Praha 1** ☎ **2242 11087**
🚇 **Staroměstská**

Galerie České Plastiky
A gallery that focuses exclusively on post-1900 Czech sculpture, including statues and busts by the great Otto Gutfreund, Jan Hána and Emanuel Kodet.
✉ **Revoluční 20, Praha 1**
☎ **2223 10684** 🚇 **Náměstí Republiky**

Galerie Jakubská
Permanent exhibition of work by modern Czech artists, and temporary exhibitions of work by artists from Russia and elsewhere.
✉ **Jakubská 4, Praha 1**
☎ **2248 27926** 🚇 **Náměstí Republiky**

Galerie Pallas
Beautifully located in the old Ungelt courtyard, this gallery concentrates on Cubist, Expressionist and Surrealist works by such 20th-century masters as Jan Čapek, Emil Filla and Antonín Procházko.
✉ **Týn 1, Praha 1** ☎ **2248 95411** 🚇 **Staromestská**

Galerie Peithner-Lichtenfels
A small, well-established gallery dealing in works by 19th- and 20th-century Czech masters, including Otto Gutfreund, Bohumil Kubišta and Toyen (Marie Čermínová).
✉ **Michalská 12, Praha 1**
☎ **2242 27680** 🚇 **Můstek**

JHB
A fascinating range of antiques and curios is on sale here, including clocks and watches, silverware, porcelain figurines and paintings.
✉ **Panská 1, Praha 1** ☎ **2222 45836** 🚇 **Můstek**

Obecní dům
The museum shop in the Municipal House picks up on the art nouveau/art deco theme with novelty items including headscarves, vases, jewellery, ties, and candlesticks (▶ 61).
✉ **Náměstí Republiky, Praha 1**
☎ **2220 02101** 🚇 **Náměstí Republiky**

Šběratel
"The Collector" just about sums up this intriguing emporium featuring lacework, dolls, erotic pictures, coins, medals, toilet sets, biscuit tins and more.
✉ **Mala Štupartská 5, Praha 1**
☎ **2248 27097** 🚇 **Náměstí Republiky**

Starožitnosti "Na Francouzské"
A small shop in Vinohrady selling rugs, porcelain statues, vases, gold and other decorative items.
✉ **Francouzská 18, Praha 2**
☎ **2242 46605** 🚇 **Náměstí Míru** 🚋 **4, 15, 22, 57**

Shopping A–Z
Prague's shops are concentrated in three main areas: the honeycomb of arcades around Václavské náměstí, Národní třída and Na příkopě – a particularly useful street with tourist information, change shops and banks. For antiques, antiquarian bookshops and craft shops, try Karlova, near the Charles Bridge. Staroměstské náměstí and the neighbouring streets are useful for gifts, postcards, guide books, T-shirts, novelties etc. Pařížská is known for its boutiques and clothing stores, and the Pavilon on Vinohradská is also worth a browse.

Department Stores & Shopping Malls

Czech Gem
The Czech national gemstone is the garnet, mostly mined in the vicinity of Teplica, about 50km northwest of Prague. Take note that fakes are common, so shop at the more reputable outlets, which include Granat ⊠ Dlouha 30, Praha 1

Bílá Labut'
The White Swan is a Czech-owned department store with men's and women's fashions, furniture, supermarket, florist, currency exchange, drugstore, gift shop and even its own branch of the ubiquitous US burger giant McDonalds.
⊠ Na poříčí 23, Praha 1
☎ 2248 11364 🚇 Florenc
🚌 24

Černa Růže
This very handily situated shopping mall showcases such designer names as Karl Lagerfeld, Pierre Cardin and Elazar Leatherware.
⊠ Na příkopě 12, Praha 1
☎ 2210 14111 🚇 Můstek

Dětsky Dům
Thoroughly re-modelled, this former communist megastore re-opened in 2004 with a better than ever selection of outlets stocking children's clothing, toys etc.
⊠ Na příkopě 15, Praha 1
☎ 2721 42401 🚇 Můstek

Dům Mody
The Fashion House has five floors of men's and women's clothing, as well as fashions for the children.
⊠ Václavské náměsti 58, Praha 2 ☎ 2961 58134 🚇 Muzeum

Kotva
Thoroughly reconstructed since the Communist era, Kotva is probably the best all-round department store in the Czech Republic. It supplies everything from designer luggage to fishing tackle.
⊠ Náměsti Republiky 1, Praha 1 ☎ 2248 01111
🚇 Náměsti Republiky

Krone
A typical European department store, with four floors and well-stocked shelves.
⊠ Václavské náměstí 21, Praha 1 ☎ 2242 30477
🚇 Můstek

Lucerna Arcade
Vaclev Havel's grandfather designed this splendid art nouveau shopping arcade where you'll now find a number of fashion boutiques and occasional shows.
⊠ Stěpánská 61/Vodičkova 36, Praha 1 🚇 Muzeum

Palác Flóra
A new kid on the block, this mall has more than 120 shops, plus cafes, restaurants and multiplex cinema.
⊠ Vinohradská 151, Praha 3
☎ 2557 41700 🚇 Flora

Pavilon
This former market hall has been restored as an attractive modern shopping mall including cafés and fashion shops.
⊠ Vinhradská 50, Praha 1
🚌 11

Tesco
This store is popular with locals and visitors alike. During the Communist era this was the Máj department store; then K-Mart took over. Now it is the British supermarket chain Tesco that has taken possession of the building and sells just about everything conceivable. There are good views of the city centre from the escalator.
⊠ Národní třída 26, Praha 1
☎ 2220 03111 🚇 Národní třída 🚌 6, 9, 18, 22, 51

Clothing, Jewellery & Accessories

Benetton
The famous international Italian designer offers the usual range of bright sweaters, jeans and other casual wear for both men and women.
✉ **Na příkopě 4, Praha 1**
☎ **2248 95460** Ⓜ **Můstek**

Bohéme
Specialist in designer Czech knitwear, also sells attractively priced leather goods and interesting accessories.
✉ **Dušni 8, Praha 1**
☎ **2248 13840** Ⓜ **Staroměstská**

Delmas
A selection of leather goods made in the Czech Republic is sold here, including back packs and suitcases. Also some Italian leatherware.
✉ **Vodičkova 36, Praha 1**
☎ **2242 39132** Ⓜ **Můstek**
🚋 **1, 9, 14, 24, 52, 53, 55, 56**

Diesel
Stylish clothes for the young and the young at heart, suitable for nightclubbing.
✉ **Národní 17, Praha 1**
☎ **2242 22444** Ⓜ **Můstek**

Fabergé
Czech representative of the world-renowned Russian jewellers, specialising in ornamental eggs; also plates, rings, necklaces etc.
✉ **Pařížská 15, Praha 1**
☎ **2223 23085**
Ⓜ **Staroměstská**

Halada
A Czech chain which sells gold and silver, pearls, diamonds and gems, all made by the Dutch wife of the proprietor.
✉ **Karlova 25, Praha 1**

☎ **2242 18643**
Ⓜ **Staroměstská**

Ivana Follová
One of the most original and creative of Czech designers, Follová produces extremely attractive dresses and blouses, many of which have been personally hand-dyed. Shoppers also come here to buy the novelty purses.
✉ **Týn 1, Praha 1** ☎ **2248 95460** Ⓜ **Staroměstská**

Marks & Spencer
Czech branch of the popular British store, specialising in mid-range men and women's clothing at accessible prices. (No food department though).
✉ **Na příkopě 19 (Myslbek Shopping Centre), Praha 1**
☎ **2242 32237** Ⓜ **Můstek**

Piano Boutique
A selection of fashionable clothing from the best-known Czech designers, including Timoure et Group, Boheme and Marcela Kotěšovcová – sold here at reasonable prices.
✉ **Vinohradská 47, Praha 2**
☎ **2222 50094** Ⓜ **Jiřího z Poděbrad** 🚋 **11**

Silver Shop
Attractive silver jewellery from around the world is sold in the Silver Shop, including rings with inlaid semi-precious stones.
✉ **Železná 4, Praha 1**
☎ **2242 21991** Ⓜ **Můstek**

Zlatnictum Frantisek Vomácka
Antique and second-hand jewellery and porcelain.
➕ **E4** ✉ **Náprstkova 9, Staré Město** ☎ **2222 22017**
Ⓜ **Národní třída**

Czech Them Out
'Hello Boys!' Everyone remembers Eva Herzigova and the Wonderbra advert, but now the celebrity model is no longer a lone Czech on the international catwalk. Most of the new generation of models, including Simona Krajinova and Tereza Maxova, were discovered by the thrusting power of the Czechoslavk Models agency, Milada Karašová. Most successful to date is Daniela Peštová, currently making $12,000 a day working for L'Oreal – she already has her own page on the Internet.

Food & Drink

Ready to Eat
Several restaurants offer takeaway and/or delivery services which may come in handy, especially if you're living in private accommodation. You can pick up a grilled chicken at Grill Bono ✉ Spálená 43, Praha 1, or something healthier, including sandwiches and soups, at Cornucopia ✉ Jungmannova 10, Praha 1 ☎ 2242 20950. Food Taxi ☎ 7771 71394; www.foodtaxi.cz operates a takeaway and delivery service, drawing on 9 restaurants and featuring Italian, Chinese and Czech dishes.

Country Life
A refuge for vegans and strict vegetarians who find themselves unable to cope with Prague's carnivorous restaurant scene. Seeds, muesli, dried food, soya products, wholewheat bread, veggie sandwiches and other items.
✉ **Melantrichova 15, Praha 1**
☎ **2242 13366**
🚇 **Staroměstská**

Cukrárna Monika
Cukrárna Monika is a small bakery which offers a beguiling selection of sweets – everything from elaborate wedding cakes to tasty ice cream sundaes.
✉ **Charvátova 11, Praha 1**
☎ **2242 11622**
🚇 **Staroměstska**

Cukrárna Simona
Small shop on Wenceslas Square, packed with sweets and chocolates. Also *Becherovka*, *Slivovice* and *Kokos* (Czech liqueurs)
✉ **Václavské náměstí 14, Praha 1** ☎ **2242 27585**
🚇 **Můstek**

Dufek
Handy mainstream Czech bakery, specialising in marzipan novelty sweetmeats (hens, cats, ducks etc.) They also sell the national liqueur, Becherovka.
✉ **Vodičkova 9, Praha 1** ☎ **No phone** 🚇 **Můstek**

Dum lahudek u Rotta
Formally a hardware store this is now one of the best delis in Prague. Choose from its vast selection of local and regional cheeses, sausages, patés, caviar and pastries.
✉ **Malé náměstí 3, Praha 1** ☎ **2242 34457** 🚇 **Staroměstská**

Fruits de France
Fruits de France changed the face of food shopping in Prague after the Velvet Revolution and stocks rarities like passion fruits and seedless grapes, as well as a varied selection of dried fruits and nuts.
✉ **Jindřišská 9, Praha 1**
☎ **2242 20304** 🚇 **Můstek**

Jan Paukert
Czech delicatessen selling Italian prosciutto, imported cheeses and other products; also well-stocked with European wines.
✉ **Národní třída 17, Praha 1**
☎ **2242 32466** 🚇 **Národní třída** 🚊 **6, 9, 18, 22, 51**

Julius Meinl
Julius Meinl is an Austrian-owned supermarket chain and stocks a wide variety of imported cheeses, fruit and vegetables, as well as other basic goods.
✉ **Náměstí Republiky 8, Praha 1** ☎ **2248 01111** 🚇 **Náměstí Republiky**

Wine Shop Ungelt
The brick-vaulted 14th-century cellar makes an atmospheric setting for the daily wine tastings; while the shop stocks quality wines from around the world.
✉ **Týnský dvůr 7, Praha 1**
☎ **2248 27501**

Zemark
Large, central grocery shop with an appetising array of salads on the delicatessen counter. Also a wide choice of Moravian wines, Bohemian *Sekt*, whiskeys, liqueurs and vodkas.
✉ **Václavské náměstí 42, Praha 1** ☎ **2242 17326**
🚇 **Můstek**

Speciality Shops

Bat'a
One of the world's most famous shoe retailers, Bat'a returned to Prague after the Velvet Revolution and continues to produce foot-wear of the very highest quality.
✉ **Václavské náměstí 6, Praha 1** ☎ **2242 18133** Ⓜ **Můstek**

Big Ben
The perfect port of call if you've forgotten to pack your holiday reading matter. Only English language books are on sale here, including guides to Prague and children's books.
✉ **Malá Štupartská 5, Praha 1** ☎ **2248 26565** Ⓜ **Náměstí Republiky**

Capriccio
This store boasts the largest selection of sheet music in Prague: more than 10,000 items in all, including jazz and classical scores – also CDs.
✉ **Újezd 15, Praha 5** ☎ **2573 20165** 🚊 **12, 27, 57**

Dům Sportu
Central shop with a comprehensive range of sportwear and sporting equipment.
✉ **Jungmannova 28, Praha 1** ☎ **2242 12347** Ⓜ **Můstek**

Knihkupectví Na Můstku
Small, but useful bookshop selling a range of art glossies and books about Prague as well as general titles.
✉ **Na Příkopě 3, Praha 1** ☎ **2242 16383** Ⓜ **Můstek**

Knihkupectví U Černé Matky Boží
Central bookshop with a good selection of maps and guide books in English and other languages.
✉ **Celetná 34, Praha 1** ☎ **2242 11155** Ⓜ **Můstek**

Kodak Express
Camera equipment including film and batteries and a 1-hour processing service.
✉ **Branches at: Ninohradská 6; Komunardů 19 and Metro Hradčanská**

Philharmonia
The official representative of the Prague Philharmonic Orchestra stocks a comprehensive range of CDs, also DVDs, videos and books at competitive prices.
✉ **Pařížská 13, Praha 1** ☎ **2223 24060** Ⓜ **Staroměstská**

The Globe Bookstore and Coffeehouse (£)
This bookstore-cum-café is a good source for English language versions of contemporary classics by writers such as Milan Kundera and Václav Havel.
✉ **Pstrosova 6, Praha 1** ☎ **2249 34203** Ⓜ **Národní třída** 🚊 **6, 9, 17, 21, 22, 23, 51, 54, 58**

Tobacco, Cigars & Pipes
An Aladdin's cave of Cuban cigars, tobacco, cigarette-lighters and pipes.
✉ **Pavilon, Vinohradská 50, Praha 2** ☎ **2242 33125** 🚊 **11**

U Jednorožce
One of Old Town Square's most distinguished historic houses, 'At the Unicorn' sells maps, guides, comics and a good selection of postcards.
✉ **Staroměstské náměstí 17, Praha 1** ☎ **2242 10606** Ⓜ **Staroměstská**

Kafka's Store
Franz Kafka's father, Hermann, ran a haberdashery business which fascinated his young son. He was notoriously rude to staff and abrupt with customers but that didn't seem to affect his business, which prospered over the years. In 1886 the store moved from Old Town Square to larger premises in Celetná 3, then 12.

Children in Prague

Tram Rides

Prague's red-and-cream trams are a familiar sight on the streets of the town and are fascinating to children who haven't seen them operating at home. The most scenic route is No 22, which winds around the Malá Strana and Hradčany.

Activities

Club Lávka

Paddle boats are available for hire below the Charles Bridge.

✉ **Novotného Lávka 1, Praha 1**
☎ **2222 20767**
🚇 **Staroměstská**

Cruises

There is a one-hour river cruise that takes you past all the familiar city landmarks, including Prague Castle, the Charles Bridge, the National Theatre and Na Kampě. Boats set off from the jetty at Čechův most on the Na Frantisku embankment.

The Exhibition Ground

In the inner suburb of Holešovice, the extensive Exhibition Grounds have an old-fashioned fun-fair, a swimming pool, the Seaworld aquarium (➤ 72) and a planetarium that presents several shows daily between 2 and 5PM.

✉ **Výstavišt Praha 7, Holešovice** ☎ **2201 03111**
🚇 **Vltavská**

Petřín Park

Petřín Park is a relaxing place to head for with the children on a warm day, after a morning's hectic sightseeing – in the castle perhaps. Take a picnic lunch with you and enjoy the wonderful views, then explore the labyrinth of mirrors in the Mirror Maze and take a ride on the funicular railway.

Pony Traps

Take a pony trap ride from Old Town Square through Josefov (summer months only).

Tram Rides (➤ panel)

Eateries

Bohemia Bagel

Filling snacks in a friendly and informal setting.

✉ **Újezd 16, Praha 1**
☎ **2573 10694**

Tramvaj II Café

You can't really miss the gleaming red and yellow tramcars permanently parked on a small island just outside the metro entrance on Wenceslas Square. For the children there's milk shakes, pizzas and apple pie to choose from, while the adults may prefer coffee or something a little stronger.

✉ **Václavské náměstí, Praha 1**
☎ **No phone** 🚇 **Můstek**

Museums, Shops, Sights and Theatres

Muzeum Dětské Kresby (Museum of Children's Pictures)

The idea is simple. Children of all ages bring their drawings and paintings to this converted baroque building near Old Town Square and hand them over to be exhibited. They can then admire the work of other children while being entertained by the adults on hand – anyone from craftsmen making toy frogs to theatre troupes, singers or ladies wearing fancy dress.

✉ **Green Frog House, 1st floor, U Radnice 13/8, Praha 1**
☎ **2242 34482** 🕐 **Tue–Sun 1–6** 🚇 **Staroměstská**

Muzeum Hraček (Toy Museum)

A treat is in store for your children at this fascinating museum set in the grounds of Prague Castle. The toy array spans 150 years and includes a collection of dolls and model houses, cars, aircraft, paddle steamers, trains, farmyards, teddy bears and dolls, robots, musical toys and tin clockwork toys. Intriguing and enjoyable for adults, too.

✉ Jiřská 6, Hradčany ☎ 2243 72294 🕐 Tue–Sun 🚋 22

Národní Technické Muzeum (National Technical Museum)

A popular venue for Czech school parties, the Transport Hall has a wonderful collection of handsome vintage cars, old trains, motorcycles and aeroplanes. For the really adventurous there is a simulated coal mine (➤ 60). There are also interesting exhibits on photography and astronomy.

✉ Kostelní 42, Praha 7 ☎ 2333 71801 🕐 Tue–Sun 9–5 🚇 Vltavská 🚋 1, 26

Shops

Games & Puzzles

Plenty of games, puzzles and brain teasers to divert and entertain.

✉ Vaclavské náměstí 38, Praha 1 ☎ 2242 28453 🚇 Můstek, Muzeum

MPH

A large store not far from the New Town Hall, specialising in model-making kits for planes, trains, ships, cars, you name it.

✉ Myslikovna 19, Praha 1 ☎ 2249 30257 🚇 Karlovo náměstí

Sparkys

Children love exploring the four floors of toys and gifts

on display here – everything from traditional wooden train sets and puppets to Star Wars death lasers.

✉ Havířská 2, Praha 1 ☎ 2242 39309 🚇 Můstek

Sights

The sights of Prague are as appealing to children as they are to adults. Some of the highlights are:
The Astronomical Clock on the Old Town Hall (➤ 22)
The Gargoyles on St Vitus's Cathedral (➤ 18)
The tiny, colourfully painted houses on Golden Lane (➤ 73)

Zoologická Zahrada (Prague Zoo)

This zoo, though nothing to write home about, is more likely to entertain children than the nearby Troja Château!

✉ U Trojského zámku 3, Troja ☎ 2961 12111 🕐 Daily 9–7 🚌 Bus 112

Theatres

Národní Divadlo Marionet (National Marionette Theatre)

It's well worth investigating the programme of productions here. The theatre has matinée, as well as evening performances (➤ 112).

✉ Žatecka 1, Praha 1 ☎ 2249 01448 🚇 Staroměstská

Spejbl and Hurvínek Theatre

Shows for children feature the comic character, Hurvínek (Spejbl is aimed at adults).

✉ Dejvická 38, Praha 6 ☎ 2243 16186 🚇 Dejvická

Playgrounds

After a museum or two, your children will probably be in the mood to stretch their legs and run around. There are small children's playgrounds all over town, for example on Masná (in the Jewish Quarter), and plenty of open spaces – Karlovo náměstí, to name just one.

Entertainment

Beethoven in Prague

Most visitors to Prague are aware of the Mozart connection, but how many know that another great composer, Ludwig van Beethoven, also came here on one occasion? The house where the 26-year-old musician stayed in 1796 (on the corner of Lázeňská and Maltézské náměstí) was then the Golden Unicorn Hotel. During his stay, Beethoven also gave a recital at Count Clam-Gallas's palace on Husova Street.

Theatres and Concert Halls

Černé Divadlo Animato (Black Light Theatre)

Pantomime with luminescent actors and props, performing under black lights. The programmes are based on well-known stories: *Don Quijote, Alice in Wonderland,* Czech fairy-tales etc. Performances begin at 8PM and take place at several different venues.

Black Light Theatre
✉ Rytířská 31, Praha 1
☎ information 2216 10173; box office 2216 10114; www. blacktheatre.cz 🚇 Můstek

Theatre Animato
✉ Na Příkopě 10, Praha 1
☎ 2222 44358 🚇 Můstek

Divadlo Metro
✉ Národní 25, Praha 1
☎ 2210 85276;
www.blacktheatreprague.cz
🚇 Národní třída

Image Theatre
✉ Pařížská 4, Praha 1 ☎ 2223 14458; www.imagetheatre.cz
🚇 Staroměstská

Ta Fantastika
✉ Karlova 8, Praha 1 ☎ 2222 21366; www.tafantastika.cz
🚇 Staroměstská

Divadlo Spirála

This theatre, set in the exhibition grounds, is used for popular musicals such as *Jesus Christ Superstar, Hair* etc.
✉ Výstaviště Praha 7, Holešovice ☎ 2201 03624
🚇 Nádraží Holešovice 🚋 5, 12, 17

Kongresové Centrum Praha (Congress Centre Prague)

The largest venue in the city hosts classical concerts, big-budget Czech-language musicals and other events.
✉ Ulice 5 května 65, Praha 4
☎ 2611 71111 🚇 Vyšehrad

Laterna Magika, Magic Lantern

A multi-media show, combining live theatre, film and dance – not as revolutionary a concept as it once was, but still popular. Performances at 5PM and 8PM.
✉ Nová Scena, Národní třída 4, Praha 1 ☎ 2249 14129 🚇
Národní třída 🚋 6, 9, 18, 22, 51

Národní Divadlo (National Theatre)

Czech National Opera performs the mainstream classical repertoire: Mozart, Verdi, Puccini, Smetana *et al.* The National Ballet Company also performs here. Performances usually start at 7PM. (► 59)
✉ Národní třída 2, Praha 1
☎ 2249 01488/01270;
www.narodni-divadlo.cz 🚇
Národní třída 🚋 6, 9, 18, 22, 51

Národní Divadlo Marionet (National Marionette Theatre)

Puppets and costumed actors perform classical operas like Mozart's *Don Giovanni* as well as some lighter fare, such as the Beatles' *Yellow Submarine.* Performances usually begin at 8PM.
✉ Žatecka 1, Praha 1
☎ 2249 01448; www.narodni-divadlo.cz 🚇 Staroměstská

Rudolfinum

The city's premier concert venue is home to the Czech Philharmonic Orchestra, the country's best ensemble. Two other excellent orchestras, the Prague

Symphony and the Prague Radio Symphony also perform here. Performances begin at 7:30PM.

✉ **Náměstí Jana Palacha, Praha 1** ☎ 2248 93111; www.rudolfinium.cz Ⓜ **Staroměstská**

Smetanova síň (Smetana Hall)

Beautifully restored venue for symphony concerts in Obecní dům.

✉ **Obecní dům, Náměstí Republiky 5, Praha 1** ☎ 2220 02336 Ⓜ **Náměstí Republiky**

Státní Opera Praha (State Opera House)

An offshoot of the National Opera Company, this troupe concentrates on the mainstream standards, virtually to the exclusion of everything else. Performances usually begin at 7PM.

✉ **Wilsonova 4, Praha 2** ☎ **information 8001 35784; box office 2242 27266; www.opera.cz** Ⓜ **Muzeum**

Stavovské Divadlo (Estates Theatre)

Mozart is performed here on a regular basis, of course, but there are also other productions, notably classical drama and occasionally ballet. Performances usually begin at 7PM.

✉ **Ovocny trh 2, Praha 1** ☎ **2242 15001/2249 01448;** www.narodni-divadlo.cz Ⓜ **Mústek**

Cinemas

There are cinemas all over Prague, with a concentration around Wenceslas Square. Most mainstream foreign films are shown with Czech

subtitles. It is best to check listings magazines for show times, but there are usually performances at around 2:30, 5 and 7:15–8. Art films are sometimes shown at the Veletržní Palác. Below is a selection of the city's cinemas:

Aero

✉ **Biskupcova 31, Praha 3** ☎ 2717 71349 🚋 **1, 9, 18, 58**

Bjásek

✉ **Náměstí Republiky 8, Praha 1** ☎ **No phone** 🚇 **Náměstí Republiky**

Biograf

✉ **U Kina 44, Praha 4** ☎ 2417 22832 🚋 **1, 3, 17, 21**

Blaník

✉ **Václavské náměstí 56, Praha 1** ☎ 2240 32111 Ⓜ **Muzeum**

Evald

✉ **Narodni 28, Praha 1** ☎ 2211 05225 Ⓜ **Národní třída**

Galaxie Multiplex

✉ **Arkalycká, Praha 4** ☎ 2679 00567 Ⓜ **Háje**

Illusion

✉ **Vinohradská 48, Praha 2** ☎ 2225 20379 Ⓜ **Jiřihoz Podebrad**

Lucerna

✉ **Vodičkova 36, Praha 1** ☎ 2242 16972 Ⓜ **Mústek**

MAT Studio

✉ **Karlovo náměstí 19, Praha 1** ☎ 2249 15765 Ⓜ **Karlovo náměstí**

Perštýn

✉ **Na Perštýné 6** ☎ 2216 68432 Ⓜ **Národní třída**

Tinsel Town

Prague has been playing host to Western film-makers ever since Miloš Forman arrived to make Amadeus in 1984. Recently more and more foreign directors have been heading for the Czech capital, which offers locations of unrivalled beauty, highly trained, home-grown film technicians and the largest studios in the region. Fortunately the income is proving hugely beneficial to the Czech film industry, now wholly reliant on private funding.

Discos, Clubs & Bars

Ticket Offices
To get hold of tickets for the theatre or other events, try one of the city's central ticket offices: **Bohemia Ticket International** ✉ Na Příkopé 16, Praha 1 ☎ 2242 27832/37727; www.bohemiaticket.cz; also at Malé náměstí 13, Praha 1; **Ticketstream** ✉ Koubkova 8, Praha 2 ☎ 2242 63049; www.ticketstream.cz, or TicketPro ✉ Salvátorská 10, Praha 1 ☎ 2963 29696/29999; www.ticketpro.cz

Discos and Clubs

AghaRTA Jazz Centrum
Local and international jazz bands perform here. There's a jazz shop on site too, which is open Mon–Fri 5PM–midnight and Sat–Sun 7PM–midnight.
✉ Krakovská 5, Praha 1
☎ 2222 21275 🕒 Daily 9–12
🚇 Muzeum

Batalion
Popular all-night venue, with live music, rock videos and big crowds. You can use the Internet here.
✉ 28 října 3, Praha 1 ☎ 2201 08147 🕒 Daily 24 hours
🚇 Můstek

Casino Hotel Ambassador
The usual selection of casino activities is offered here, including roulette, black jack, punto banco, poker, craps and slot machines.
✉ Václavské náměstí 5-7, Praha 1 ☎ 2241 93681
🕒 Daily 24 hours 🚇 Můstek

Jazz Club Železná
A reliable, mainstream jazz club in the heart of the Old Town.
✉ Železná 16, Praha 1
☎ 2423 9697 🚇 Můstek

Klub Lavka
This vast entertainments complex on the Vltava has a riverside terrace where you can enjoy a drink from the cocktail bar, where tequilas are a speciality. Other attractions include indoor and outdoor dining spaces, a theatre, dance floors and an internet café.
✉ Novotného lavka 1, Praha 1
☎ 2222 22156
🚇 Staroměstská 🚌 17, 18

Lucerna Music Bar
A popular traditional venue, which specialises in Czech pop, Beatles and Rolling Stones revivals and covers bands.
✉ Vodičkova 36, Praha 1
☎ 2242 17108 🕒 Daily
7PM–6AM, concerts at 9PM
🚇 Můstek 🚌 3, 9, 14, 24, 52, 53, 55, 56

Red Hot & Blues
Jazz and blues club with live bands every night, frequented by ex-pats and tourists. Also has a popular Tex-Mex-style restaurant – serving some of the best nachos in town – with courtyard seating when the weather is favourable
(► 95).
✉ Jakubska 12, Praha 1
☎ 2223 14639

Reduta Jazz Club and Rock Café
Swing, traditional, Dixieland and many other varieties of jazz, played by Czech bands.
✉ Národní třída 20, Praha 1
☎ 2249 33487 🕒 Daily 9PM (concerts) 🚇 Národní třída
🚌 6, 9, 18, 22, 51

Roxy
This popular Josefov club attracts a loyal clientele that appreciates its run-down look and relaxed atmosphere.
✉ Dlouhá 33, Praha 1
☎ 2248 26296 🕒 Daily
5PM–2:30AM 🚇 Staroměstská

Ungelt Jazz and Blues Club
The name says it all – quintets, fusion bands, big bands etc. All featuring prominent Czech artists.
✉ Týn 2, Praha 1 ☎ 2248 95748 🕒 Daily from 8PM
🚇 Staroměstská

U Staré Paní

'At the Old Lady' is a hotel, restaurant and jazz club with live bands.

- ✉ Michalská 9, Praha 1
- ☎ 603 551 680 🕐 Daily 4PM–4AM 🚇 Staroměstská

Bars

Banana Café

Situated in the same building as La Provence restaurant, this is one of Prague's trendiest establishments. DJs and occasional live shows.

- ✉ Štupartská 9, Praha 1
- ☎ 2248 16695
- 🚇 Staroměstská

Chateau L'enfer Rouge

Open until 5AM, this bar is almost always full to the brim and always lively. Loud music.

- ✉ Jakubská 2, Praha 1
- ☎ 2223 16328
- 🚇 Staroměstská

Konvikt

Traditional pub serving home grown and imported beers on draught. Also hearty Czech fare.

- ✉ Bartolomějska 11, Praha 1
- ☎ 2242 31971 🚇 Národní třída

Ocean Drive

Shades of Key West and other Florida locations in this trendy nightspot specialising in cocktails.

- ✉ V Kolkovně 7, Praha 1
- ☎ 2248 19089
- 🚇 Staroměstská

Pod loubín

Popular with ex-pats in the know, this neighbourhood bar on the airport road, serves Pilsner Urquell on draught along with filling, temptingly-priced Czech pub grub.

- ✉ Evropská 26, Praha 6
- ☎ 2333 26097
- 🚇 Dejvická 🚌 2, 20, 26, 51

U Dvou Koček

Pilsner Urquell and live music nightly are the attractions of this traditional Czech pub.

- ✉ Uhelný trh 10, Praha 1
- ☎ 2242 29982

U Fleků

Founded in 1499, this famous historic pub serves a unique dark beer of the same name. You can drink it indoors or in the huge beer garden.

- ✉ Křemencova 11, Praha 1
- ☎ 2249 15118 🚇 Karlovo náměstí

U Medviku

A traditional pub selling Budvar beer and light meals. The garden is open in summer.

- ✉ Na Perštýně 7, Praha 1
- ☎ 2242 20930 🚇 Národní třída

U Zlatého Tygra

The beer sold in this most traditional of pubs comes direct from the 13th-century cellars. Václav Havel brought the US President Bill Clinton here when he visited Prague in 1994 (▶ panel).

- ✉ Husova 17, Praha 1 ☎ 2242 29020 🚇 Můstek

Zlatá hvězda

One of a crop of sport bars springing up in Prague at the moment. Apart from live sport on TV, this one serves draught Gambrinus at bargain basement prices.

- ✉ Ve smečkach 12, Praha 1
- ☎ 2962 22292 🚇 Muzeum

U Zlatého Tygra

The no-frills beer hall is usually packed with Prague die-hards addicted to the golden nectar. To find a seat say *Je tu volno?* (Is this space free?) and wait to be served. Pilsner Urquell is the only beer available, delivered uniformly in half-litre measures. Each glass is marked on your tab and you can also order traditional Czech snacks like Prague ham with horseradish sauce. When you're ready to go, say *Platit prosím* – don't expect an itemised bill, you won't be overcharged.

What's on When

Smaller Venues

Many of Prague's palaces and historic churches are used for concerts, especially in the summer. These events are not only enjoyable in themselves but also allow visitors to see some splendid interiors not otherwise open to the public. Some venues to look out for are: the Chapel of Mirrors in the Klementinum, the Nostitz Palace, Lichtenstein Palace, Lobkowicz Palace, Clam-Gallas Palace, Bertramka, Bethlehem Chapel, St Agnes's Convent, St George's Basilica and the House at the Stone Bell.

19 January

Anniversary of the death of Jan Palach:
The suicide of the young student protester in 1968, in protest at the Soviet invasion of Czechoslovakia, is commemorated at his memorial on Wenceslas Square and at Olšany Cemetery.

March

International Music Festival:
A series of classical and contemporary concerts is performed in venues all over the city throughout the month.

30 April

Witches' Night:
A bonfire held on Petřín Hill celebrates the traditional end of winter and the birth of spring.

Early May

Prague Spring:
A three-week programme of classical music and dance, performed in churches, palaces and concert halls around Prague. The celebrations begin with a procession from Smetana's grave in Vyšehrad to his namesake concert hall in Obecní Dům, where a celebratory performance of Ma Vlast is given.

June

Dance Prague:
An international festival of modern dance with a variety of events held at indoor and outdoor venues throughout the city.

August

International Table Tennis Tournament.

September

Prague Autumn:
A two-week music festival is led by the city's orchestras and internationally renowned soloists.

October

Mozart in Prague:
A month-long music festival commemorating the composer's visit to the city in 1787.

17 November

Anniversary of the Velvet Revolution:
A commemoration and wreath-laying ceremony conducted on Wenceslas Square and Národní (although there has been much concern voiced by citizens recently about the poor attendance at this event).

December

Christmas market on Old Town Square:
Throughout the festive season a giant Christmas tree lights up the centre of the square, while the space around it is crammed with market stalls selling carved toys, bobbin lace, ceramics, glass figurines, Christmas ornaments and tasty gingerbread cakes, barbecued sausages and mulled wine. Entertainment is provided by musicians, dancers, jugglers and other performers.

Practical Matters

Above: *new banknote*
Right: *Prague telephone*

TIME DIFFERENCES

GMT 12 noon	Prague 1PM	Germany 1PM	USA (NY) 7AM	Netherlands 1PM	Spain 1PM

BEFORE YOU GO

WHAT YOU NEED

● Required ○ Suggested ▲ Not required	Some countries require a passport to remain valid for a minimum period (usually at least six months) beyond the date of entry – contact their consulate or embassy or your travel agent for details.	UK	Germany	USA	Netherlands	Spain
Passport/National Identity Card		●	●	●	●	●
Visa (Regulations can vary – check before your journey)		▲	▲	▲	▲	▲
Onward or Return Ticket		▲	▲	▲	▲	▲
Health Inoculations		▲	▲	▲	▲	▲
Health Documentation (► 123, Health)		●	●	●	●	●
Travel Insurance		○	○	○	○	○
Driving Licence (national)		●	●	●	●	●
Car Insurance Certificate		●	●	●	●	●
Car Registration Document		●	●	●	●	●

WHEN TO GO

Prague

■ High season
□ Low season

-1°C	0°C	4°C	9°C	14°C	17°C	19°C	18°C	14°C	9°C	4°C	0°C
JAN	FEB	MAR	APR	MAY	JUN	JUL	AUG	SEP			

Wet   Cloud   Sun   Sunshine & showers

TOURIST OFFICES

In the UK
Czech Tourist Authority,
The Czech Centre,
95 Great Portland Street,
London W1N 5RA
☎ 020 7291 9920
Fax: 020 7436 8300

In the USA
Czech Tourist Authority,
1109–1111 Madison Avenue,
New York
NY 10028
☎ 212/288 0830
Fax: 212/288 0971

POLICE 158

AMBULANCE 155

FIRE 150

WHEN YOU ARE THERE

ARRIVING

Czechoslovak Airlines – ČSA (☎ 2401 04111) operates direct scheduled flights to Prague from Britain, mainland Europe and North America. Flight time from London is two hours. Prague is connected by rail to all main European capitals (➤ 121, Public Transport).

Praha Ruzyně Airport Kilometres to city centre	**Journey times**	
● ➤ **20 kilometres**	🚌	40 minutes
	🚐	35 minutes
	🚗	20–25 minutes

Praha Hlavní Station In city centre	**Journey times**	
● ➤	🚌	on metro line C
	🚐	available
	🚗	available

MONEY

The monetary unit of the Czech Republic is the Koruna česká (Kč) – or Czech crown – which is divided into 100 haléř (h) – or heller – though you will not find many of the latter in Prague. There are coins of 10, 20 and 50 hellers and 1, 2, 5, 10, 20 and 50 crowns. Banknotes come in 20, 50, 100, 200, 500, 1,000 and 5,000 crowns. Money may be changed at the airport, in banks (➤ 120, Opening Hours), major hotels, Čedok offices, and in the centre of Prague at exchange offices. It is an offence to change money through street black-market money dealers; in any case, they rarely offer an attractive rate.

TIME

🕐 The Czech Republic is on Central European Time (GMT+1), but from late March, when clocks are put forward one hour, until late October, Czech Summer Time (GMT+2) operates.

CUSTOMS

 YES

Duty Free Limits:
Alcohol – spirits: 1L *and* wine: 2L
Cigarettes: 200 *or*
Cigarillos: 100 *or*
Cigars: 50 *or*
Tobacco: 250gms *or*
a proportionate combination of the above tobacco products.
You must be 18 and over to benefit from the alcohol and tobacco allowance.
Perfume: 50ml *or*
Toilet water: 250ml
Gifts: not in excess of 3,000Kč per person.
Fuel: 10L in a spare can (for personal use).

 NO

Drugs, firearms, ammunition, offensive weapons, obscene material, unlicensed animals.

CONSULATES

 UK
☎ 257 402 226

 Germany
☎ 257 113 111

 **USA**
☎ 257 530 663

 Netherlands
☎ 224 312 190

 Spain
☎ 224 311 441

WHEN YOU ARE THERE

TOURIST OFFICES

Czech Tourist Authority
(Česká centrála cestovního ruchu)
● ✉ Vinohradská 46
12041 Praha 2
☎ 2258 0611, fax 2258 0711;
www.czechtourism.com

Prague Information Service
(Pražská informační služba PIS)
● ✉ Staroměstská radnice
(Old Town Hall),
Staroměstské náměstí,
Praha 1
☎ 2244 82202;
www.prague-info.cz
🚇 Staroměstská
🕐 Mon–Fri 8–7

● ✉ Praha hlavní nádraží
(Main Railway Station)
Wilsonova, Praha 1
🚇 Hlavní nádraží
🕐 Apr–Oct Mon–Fri 9–7,
Sat–Sun 9–4; Nov–Mar
Mon–Fri 9–6, Sat–Sun 9–3

● ✉ Malostranská Mostecká
vez, (Lesser Town Tower),
Mostecká, Praha 1
🚇 Malostranská
🕐 Apr–Oct daily 10–6

Tourist Information Centre
● ✉ Celetná, Praha 1
☎ 2244 91764;
www.aroundprague.cz
🚇 Staroměstská
🕐 Daily 9–8

NATIONAL HOLIDAYS

J	F	M	A	M	J	J	A	S	O	N	D
1		(1)	(1)	2		2			1		3

1 Jan	New Year's Day
Mar/Apr	Easter Monday
1 May	May Day
8 May	Liberation Day
5 Jul	St Cyril and St Method Day
6 Jul	Jan Hus Day
28 Sep	Czech Statehood Day
28 Oct	Independence Day
17 Nov	Democracy Day
24–25 Dec	Christmas Eve/Day
26 Dec	St Stephen's Day

Restaurants, museums and other tourist attractions
tend to stay open on these days.

OPENING HOURS

○ Shops	● Castles/chateaux
● Offices	● Museums
● Banks	● Pharmacies

8AM	9AM	10AM	NOON	1PM	2PM	3PM	4PM	5PM	6PM

☐ Day	☐ Midday
☐ Evening	

Some shops close for lunch. Most shops open
Saturday until 12 noon or 1PM. Food shops open from
7AM; department stores and large shopping centres
open until 8PM (4PM Saturday); gift shops generally
10AM–10PM. Outside Prague centre, shops close on
Sunday. Some pharmacies open 24 hours. Banks vary,
some open Saturday morning. Museums and art
galleries usually open from 9/10AM to 5/6PM; they are
closed Mondays. Castles, chateaux and other
historical monuments open daily (except Monday)
May to September and weekends in April and
October, but may be closed other times; please check.

DRIVE ON THE RIGHT

TOILETS CHARGE

PUBLIC TRANSPORT

Internal Flights Czechoslovak Airlines (ČSA), Revoluční 1, Praha 1 (☎ 2201 04111), and a variety of other carriers link Prague with Brno and Ostrava. Though not cheap, especially when compared with the train or bus, they are useful when you want to get somewhere quickly.

Trains Czech Railways (Československé Stání Dráhy, ČSD, ☎ 2242 24200; English language 22461 14030) run *rychlík* that stop only at major towns and *osobní* calling at every station. Services to north and east Bohemia depart from Masarykovo nádraží; routes to the south are from Smíchovské nádraží.

River Boats From April to September cruise boats chug up and down the Vltava River, as far as Troja Château in the north of Prague and Slapy Lake in the south. The Prague Steamship Company (Pražská paroplavební služba, ☎ 2493 00017; www. paroplavba.cz) is the main operator. Most tours start from Paroplavební pier.

Metro Prague's metro is clean, fast and cheap. There are three lines: A (green), B (yellow), C (red). Trains run 5AM to 12 midnight, every 2 minutes peak times (5 to 10 minutes other times). The letter 'M' with a downward arrow marks a station entrance. For information (also trams and buses) ☎ 2961 91817.

Trams/Buses After the metro, trams (*tramvaje*) are the fastest way of getting around Prague. There are 23 lines running every 6 to 8 minutes peak times (10 to 15 minutes other times). Buses (*autobusy*) are of little use as they mainly keep out of the centre. There is one ticket for the metro, tram and bus.

CAR RENTAL

A car is not really neces- sary for Prague as much of the city centre is pedestrianised. Car rental is, however, easy to arrange but can be quite expensive. Shop around, many small local firms charge less than well known names. Dvořák Rent a Car (☎ 2249 26260).

TAXIS

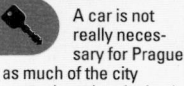

Taxis abound in Prague. An unoccupied taxi has a lit-up sign and may be hailed on the street or hired from a taxi rank. Registered taxis should have a meter clearly displayed. Beware of drivers who charge what they feel like, you have the right to a printed receipt.

DRIVING

Speed limit on motorways (annual toll payable): **130kph.** Minimum limit: **50kph**

Speed limit on country roads: **90kph** (on level crossings: **30kph**)

Speed limit on urban roads: **50kph**

Must be worn in front seats – and rear seats where fitted. Under 12s may not travel in the front seat.

Don't drink *any* alcohol if driving. The allowed blood/alcohol level is zero and penalties are severe.

Petrol (*benzín*) is sold in leaded form as *special* (91 octane) and super (96 octane). Unleaded petrol comes as *natural* (95 octane) and *super plus* (98 octane), the latter is available only at larger petrol stations. Diesel (*nafta*) is also available. In Prague, filling stations are few and far between, but some open 24 hours.

ÚAMK, the Czech automobile club, operates a 24-hour nationwide breakdown service on the same terms as your own motoring club at home (non-members pay in full), ☎ 0123 (123 in Prague) or 154 from mobile phones. On motorways use emergency phones (every 2km) to summon help.

Ruler markings:

CENTIMETRES 0 1 2 3 4 5 6 7 8

INCHES 0 1 2 3

PERSONAL SAFETY

Prague is a comparatively safe city, though petty crime is on the increase, especially around Wenceslas Square, Old Town Square, Charles Bridge and the Castle. Report any loss or theft to the *Městská policie* (municipal police) – black uniforms.

- Watch your bag in tourist areas, on the metro/trams.
- Never leave anything of value on show in your car.
- Deposit your passport and valuables in the hotel safe.
- Avoid walking alone in dark alleys at night.

Police assistance:
☎ **158**
from any call box

TELEPHONES

There are public telephones on the street and near metro stations. Older orange phones, accepting only 1Kč coins, are solely for local calls. Grey phones take 1, 2, 5 and 10Kč coins. In Prague there are an increasing number of phonecard (*Telefonní karta*) booths. Buy cards for 100, 190 and 280Kč from post offices, tobacconists and newsagents. The code for Prague is 02.

International Dialling Codes

From Czech Republic to:	
UK:	00 44
Germany:	00 49
USA:	00 1
Netherlands:	00 31
Spain:	00 34

POST

Post Offices
Post Offices have distinctive orange *Pošta* signs outside. The main post office at Jindřišská 14, Nové Město is open 24 hours. There are several branches in the city which are open 8AM–7PM (12 noon Sat) and closed Sun.
☎ 2422 8856.

ELECTRICITY

The power supply in the Czech Republic is 220 volts.

Plugs are of the two-round-pin variety, so an adaptor is needed for most non-Continental European appliances and a voltage transformer for appliances operating on 100–120 volts.

TIPS/GRATUITIES

Yes ✓ No ✗		
Hotels	✗	
Restaurants	✓	10%
Cafés	✓	10%
Taxis	✓	10%
Tour guides	✓	(20Kč)
Porters	✓	(40Kč)
Usherettes	✗	
Hairdressers	✓	10%
Cloakroom attendants	✓	(2Kč)
Toilets	✓	(2Kč)

PHOTOGRAPHY
What to photograph: after years of secret police lurking on every street corner you are now free to photograph almost anywhere.
Where to buy film: Staré Město (Old Town) and Malá Strana (Lesser Quarter) have numerous small shops selling Western film. Avoid Czech colour film as you may not be able to get it processed outside the country.
Where to get film developed: photo shops are all over the tourist areas so finding a place to get your photos developed should not be a problem.

HEALTH

Insurance
Emergency medical treatment is free to foreign visitors to the Czech Republic. EU Nationals are entitled to additional medical care (show passport). Medical insurance is still advised. US visitors should check their insurance coverage.

Dental Services
Dental treatment must be paid for. If you require urgent treatment the American Dental Associates, (✉ V celnící, Nové mesto ☎ 2211 81121) offer a 24-hour emergency service to visitors.

Sun Advice
The sun is not a real problem in Prague. June to August is the sunniest (and hottest) period but there are often thundery showers to cool things down. If the summer sun is fierce, apply a sunscreen and wear a hat, or visit a museum.

Drugs
Pharmacies (*lékárnat* or *apothéka*) are the only places to sell over-the-counter medicines. They also dispense many drugs (*leky*) normally available only on prescription in other Western countries.

Safe Water
It is not advisable to drink tap water as it is loaded with toxins and is heavily chlorinated. Bottled water is available everywhere. The still table water (*Stolní pitní voda*) is the most common.

CONCESSIONS

Students/Youths Holders of an International Identity Card (ISIC) are entitled to a 50 per cent reduction on admission to Prague's museums Student cards also offer reductions on international trains, though not on domestic public transport. The ČKM (Czech Youth Travel Agency), Žitna 12, Praha 2 (☎ 22491 15767), specialises in cheap travel for young people and students in and outside the Czech Republic. Its branch at Jindřišská 28, Praha 1 (☎ 2242 30218) issues ISICs.

Senior Citizens There are no special concessions for senior citizens. However, Saga, who organise holidays for over 50s, have trips to Prague. Contact: Saga Holidays, Saga Building, Middelburg Square, Folkestone, Kent CT20 1AZ, UK (☎ 0800 414383).

CLOTHING SIZES

Czech Republic	UK	Rest of Europe		
46	36	46	36	
48	38	48	38	
50	40	50	40	
52	42	52	42	Suits
54	44	54	44	
56	46	56	46	
41	7	41	8	
42	7.5	42	8.5	
43	8.5	43	9.5	
44	9.5	44	10.5	Shoes
45	10.5	45	11.5	
46	11	46	12	
37	14.5	37	14.5	
38	15	38	15	
39/40	15.5	39/40	15.5	
41	16	41	16	Shirts
42	16.5	42	16.5	
43	17	43	17	
34	8	34	6	
36	10	36	8	
38	12	38	10	
40	14	40	12	Dresses
42	16	42	14	
44	18	44	16	
38	4.5	38	6	
38	5	38	6.5	
39	5.5	39	7	
39	6	39	7.5	Shoes
40	6.5	40	8	
41	7	41	8.5	

WHEN DEPARTING

- Contact the airline at least 72 hours before departure to reconfirm your booking to prevent being 'bumped' from that plane because of over-allocation.
- There is an airport departure tax which is normally included in the cost of the ticket.
- Antiques can only be exported with a certificate, issued by the National Museum or National Gallery, indicating the object is not of Czech national heritage.

The official language of the Czech Republic is Czech (Český) – a highly complex western Slav tongue. Czech sounds and looks daunting, but apart from a few special letters, each letter and syllable is pronounced as it is written – the key is always to stress the first syllable of a word.

Any attempt to speak Czech will be heartily appreciated although English is spoken by many involved in the tourist trade. Below are a few Czech words that may be helpful.

hotel	*hotel*	toilet	*záchod/WC*
room	*pokoj*	bath	*koupelnoou*
I would like a room	*potřebuji pokoje*	shower	*sprcha*
... single/double	*... jednolůžjový/ dvoulůžkový*	cold/hot water	*studená/teplá voda*
... for one night	*... na jednu noc*	towel	*ručník*
how much per night?	*kolik stojí jedna noc?*	soap	*mýdlo*
		room number	*číslo pokoje*
reservation	*reservaci*	key	*klíč*
breakfast	*snídaně*		

bank	*banku*	cheap	*levný*
post office	*pošta*	expensive	*drahý*
foreign exchange	*směnárna*	free (no charge)	*zdarma*
Czech crown	*koruna česká (kč)*	more	*více*
heller	*haléř*	less	*méně*
credit card	*credit card*	the bill	*účet*
how much?	*kolik?*	it's a rip off!	*to je zlodějina!*

restaurant	*restaurace*	lunch	*oběd*
coffee house	*kavárna*	dinner	*večeře*
pub	*hospoda*	starter	*předkrm*
wine bar	*vinárna*	main course	*hlavní jídlo*
table	*stůl*	dish of the day	*nabídka dne*
menu	*jídelní lístek*	dessert	*moučník*
fixed-price menu	*standardní menu*	waiter	*číšník*
wine list	*nápojový lístek*	waitress	*servírka*

aeroplane	*letadlo*	pleasure steamer	*parník*
airport	*letiště*	small boat	*lodička*
train	*vlak*	ticket	*lístek*
train station	*nádraží*	... single/return	*jednosměrnou/ zpáteční*
metro station	*stanice*		
bus	*autobus*	... first/second class	*první/druhou třídu*
bus station	*autobusové nádraží*	ticket office	*pokladna*
tram	*tramvaj*	seat reservation	*místenka*
bus/tram stop	*zastávka*		

yes	*ano*	excuse me	*promiňte*
no	*ne*	sorry	*pardon*
please	*prosím*	help!	*pomoc!*
thank you	*děkuji*	today	*dnes*
hello	*ahoj*	yesterday	*včera*
goodbye	*na shledanou*	tomorrow	*zítra*
good morning	*dobré ráno*	open	*otevřeno*
goodnight	*dobrou noc*	closed	*zavřeno*

INDEX

INDEX

Acknowledgements

The Automobile Association wishes to thank the following photographers, libraries, associations and museums for their assistance in the preparation of this book: **MARY EVANS PICTURE LIBRARY** 10; **MRI BANKERS' GUIDE TO FOREIGN CURRENCY** 119; **ROBERT HARDING PICTURE LIBRARY** 89; **HULTON GETTY** 14; **NATIONAL GALLERY OF PRAGUE** 26

The remaining photographs are held in the Association's own library (**AA PHOTO LIBRARY**) with contributions from: **S** McBRIDE 55; **C** SAWYER 2, 5a, 5b, 13, 17, 18, 21, 20/1, 22, 25, 27, 31, 33, 35, 38, 46, 49, 54, 57, 60a, 60b, 64, 66b, 68, 70, 72, 73a, 73b, 74, 75, 85; **A** SOUTER 1, 15b, 16, 24, 41, 44, 47, 52, 61, 62, 63a; **J** WYAND front cover (a) urn, 6a, 7, 8, 9, 11, 12, 12/3, 15a, 19, 27b, 28, 29, 32, 34, 36, 37a, 37b, 39a, 39b, 42, 43, 45, 48, 50, 51, 55a, 55b, 56, 58, 59, 65, 66a, 67, 69, 71, 77, 78, 78/9, 79, 80, 81, 82, 83, 84, 86, 87a, 87b, 88, 90, 91a, 91b, 117a, 117b, 122a, 122b, 122c, 129

Authors' Acknowledgements

The authors would like to thank the AVE Travel Agency, the Prague Information Service (PIS), the National Gallery in Prague, and the Information offices in Český Krumlov, Kutná Hora, Plzeň, Tábor and Třeboň for their assistance with this book.

Contributors: Copy editor: Nia Williams **Page Layout:** The Company of Designers
Verifier: Teresa Fisher **Researcher (Practical Matters):** Colin Follett **Indexer:** Marie Lorimer
Revision management: Apostrophe S Limited

Dear Essential Traveller

**Your comments, opinions and recommendations are very
important to us. So please help us to improve our travel
guides by taking a few minutes to complete this simple
questionnaire.**

*You do not need a stamp (unless posted outside the UK). If you do not want to cut this page
from your guide, then photocopy it or write your answers on a plain sheet of paper.*

Send to: **The Editor, AA World Travel Guides,
FREEPOST SCE 4598, Basingstoke RG21 4GY.**

Your recommendations…

We always encourage readers' recommendations for restaurants, nightlife
or shopping – if your recommendation is used in the next edition of the
guide, we will send you a *FREE* AA *Essential* **Guide** of your choice.
Please state below the establishment name, location and your reasons
for recommending it.

_____

_____

_____

_____

Please send me **AA *Essential*** _____

About this guide…

Which title did you buy?
    AA *Essential* _____

Where did you buy it?_____

When? m m / y y

Why did you choose an AA *Essential* Guide? _____

_____

_____

_____

_____

Did this guide meet your expectations?
    Exceeded ☐   Met all ☐   Met most ☐   Fell below ☐

Please give your reasons_____

_____

_____

_____

continued on next page…

Were there any aspects of this guide that you particularly liked? ________

____

____

Is there anything we could have done better? ________________

____

____

About you...

Name (*Mr/Mrs/Ms*) ________________________

Address ________________________________

____

________________ Postcode ________________

Daytime tel nos ________________________

Please only give us your mobile phone number if you wish to hear from us about other products and services from the AA and partners by text or mms.

Which age group are you in?

Under 25 ☐ 25–34 ☐ 35–44 ☐ 45–54 ☐ 55–64 ☐ 65+ ☐

How many trips do you make a year?

Less than one ☐ One ☐ Two ☐ Three or more ☐

Are you an AA member? Yes ☐ No ☐

About your trip...

When did you book? m m / y y When did you travel? m m / y y

How long did you stay? ________________________

Was it for business or leisure? ____________________

Did you buy any other travel guides for your trip?

If yes, which ones? ________________________

Thank you for taking the time to complete this questionnaire. Please send it to us as soon as possible, and remember, you do not need a stamp (*unless posted outside the UK*).

Happy Holidays!

The information we hold about you will be used to provide the products and services requested and for identification, account administration, analysis, and fraud/loss prevention purposes. More details about how that information is used is in our privacy statement, which you'll find under the heading "Personal Information" in our terms and conditions and on our website: www.theAA.com. Copies are also available from us by post, by contacting the Data Protection Manager at AA, Southwood East, Apollo Rise, Farnborough, Hampshire GU14 OJW.

We may want to contact you about other products and services provided by us, or our partners (by mail, telephone) but please tick the box if you DO NOT wish to hear about such products and services from us by mail or telephone. ☐

The Atlas

Glasses filled with some of the strong local beer

www.theAA.com
The Automobile Association's website offers comprehensive and up-to-the-minute information covering AA-approved hotels, guest houses and B&Bs, restaurants and pubs in the UK; airport parking, insurance, European breakdown cover, European motoring advice, a ferry planner, European route planner, overseas fuel prices, a bookshop and much more.

www.aaa.com
AAA's website offers comprehensive information covering AAA-approved hotels and restaurants in the US. In addition, AAA can assist US citizens with obtaining a passport, reservations and tickets for cruise, tour, motorcoach, rail and air travel. AAA provides information on independent or escorted tours for individuals or groups and offers benefits on cruises, tours and travel packages.

The Foreign and Commonwealth Office Country advice, traveller's tips, before you go information, checklists and more.
www.fco.gov.uk

Website of the Czech Tourist Board.
www.czechtourism.com

GENERAL
UK Passport Service
www.ukpa.gov.uk

US passport information
www.travel.state.gov

Health Advice for Travellers
www.doh.gov.uk/traveladvice

BBC – Holiday
www.bbc.co.uk/holiday

The Full Universal Currency Converter
www.xe.com/ucc/full.shtml

Flying with Kids
www.flyingwithkids.com

Lively, up-to-date information about what's on, things to see and do, flights, even Prague cricket! There's an A–Z sightseeing guide too.
www.allpraha.com

Official website of Prague. News stories and features on the Czech Republic as well as the city, cultural events and practical information on planning your trip.
www.radio.cz

What to do with your children in Prague. Plenty of information about where to find playgrounds etc.
www.jasoncholt.com/prague

Cultural information, excursions, tours and tickets.
www.aroundprague.cz

Website of the Czech foreign ministry. Interesting factual information on everything from embassies to the weather.
www.czech.cz

The Prague Information Service offers online booking, cultural news, tips, photos, virtual tours and a wealth of general and practical information.
www.prague-info.cz

Click on Czech Republic, then Prague for a lively text, full of suggestions on accommodation, shopping, entertainment, sightseeing etc. Currency converter.
www.inyourpocket.com/prague

TRAVEL
www.cheapflights.co.uk
www.thisistravel.co.uk
www.ba.com
www.worldairportguide.com

The website of Czech railways is worth consulting before you venture out on an excursion. The English and German language sites are under construction but timetable information is available.
www.cdrail.cz

Motorway Dálnice		Autobahn Autoroute
Road with four lanes Čtyřstopá silnice		Vierspurige Straße Route à quatre voies
Thoroughfare Průjezdní silnice		Durchgangsstraße Route de transit
Main road Hlavní silnice		Hauptstraße Route principale
Other roads Ostatní silnice		Sonstige Straßen Autres routes
One-way street - Information Jednosměrná ulice - Informace	→ **i**	Einbahnstraße - Information Rue à sens unique - Information
Pedestrian zone Pěší zóna		Fußgängerzone Zone piétonne
Main railway with station Hlavní zelěznice s stanicí		Hauptbahn mit Bahnhof Chemin de fer principal avec gare
Landing place Přístaviště		Anlegestelle Embarcadère
Underground Metro	· · **ↃMↃ** · ·	U-Bahn Métro
Tramway Tramvaj		Straßenbahn Tramway
Church of interest - Other church Zajímavý kostel - Ostatní kostel		Sehenswerte Kirche - Sonstige Kirche Église remarquable - Autre église
Synagogue Synagoga		Synagoge Synagogue
Hotel Hotel	**H**	Hotel Hôtel
Youth hostel Noclehárna mládeže	▲	Jugendherberge Auberge de jeunesse
Monument - Police station Pomník - Policie		Denkmal - Polizeistation Monument - Poste de police
Tower - Radio tower Věž - Rozhlasová věž		Turm - Funkturm Tour - Tour radio
Hospital - Post office Nemocnice - Poštovní úřad		Krankenhaus - Postamt Hôpital - Bureau de poste
Built-up area, public building Zastavěná plocha, veřejná budova		Bebaute Fläche, öffentliches Gebäude Zone bâtie, bâtiment public
Industrial area Průmyslová plocha		Industriegelände Zone industrielle
Park, forest Park, les		Park, Wald Parc, bois
Vineyard Vinice		Weinberg Vignoble

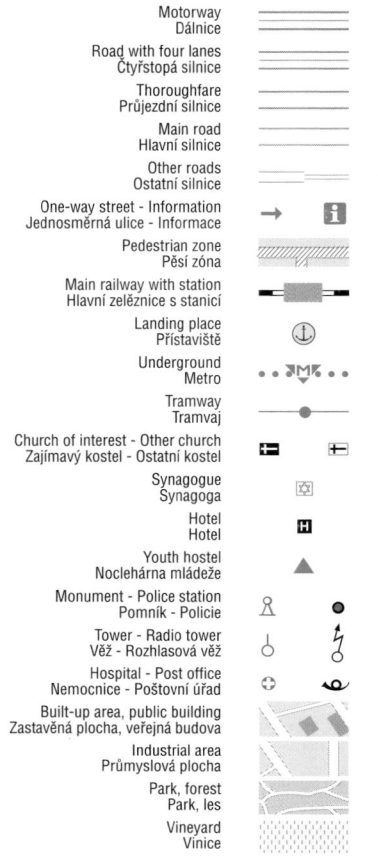

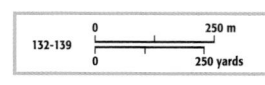

132-139
```
0                 250 m
0                 250 yards
```

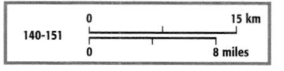

140-151
```
0                 15 km
0                 8 miles
```

Maps © Mairs Geographischer Verlag / Falk Verlag, 73751 Ostfildern

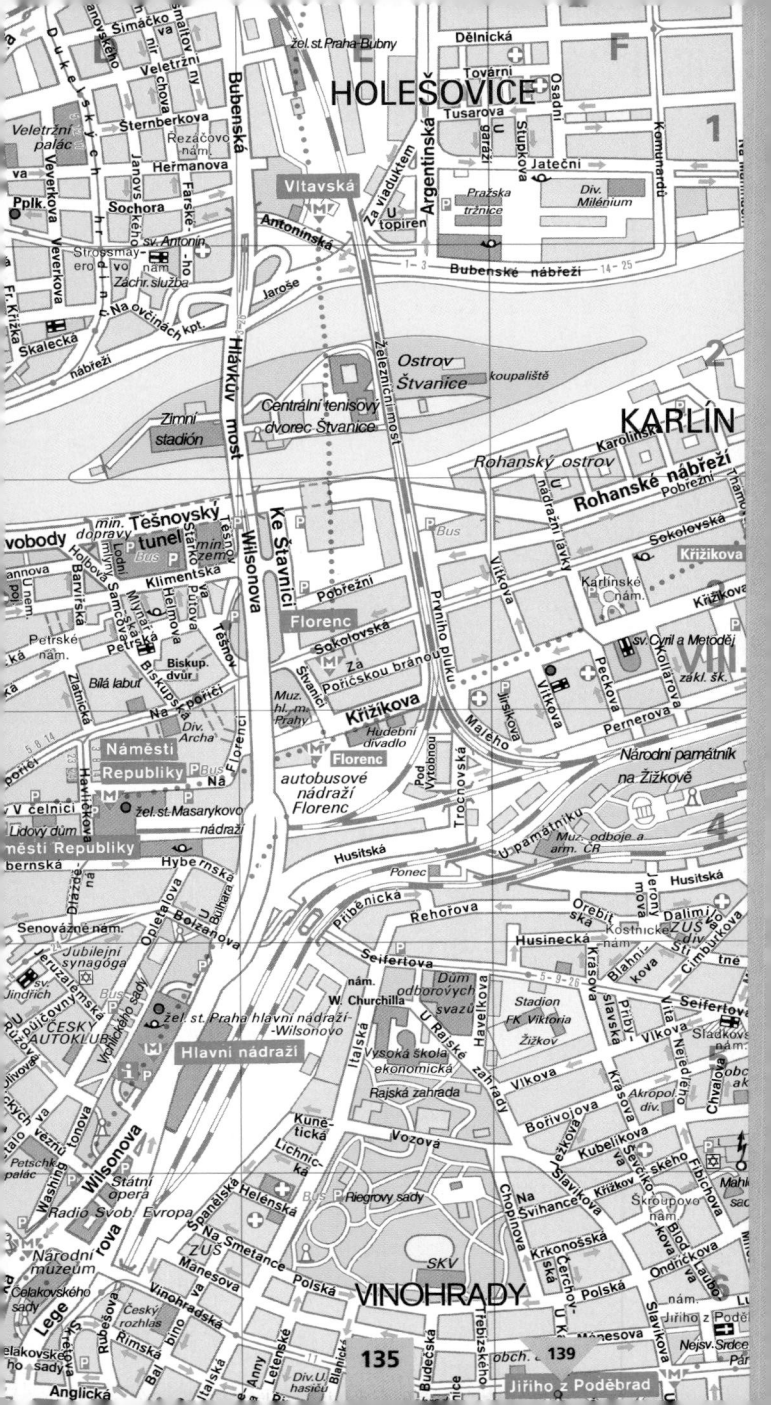

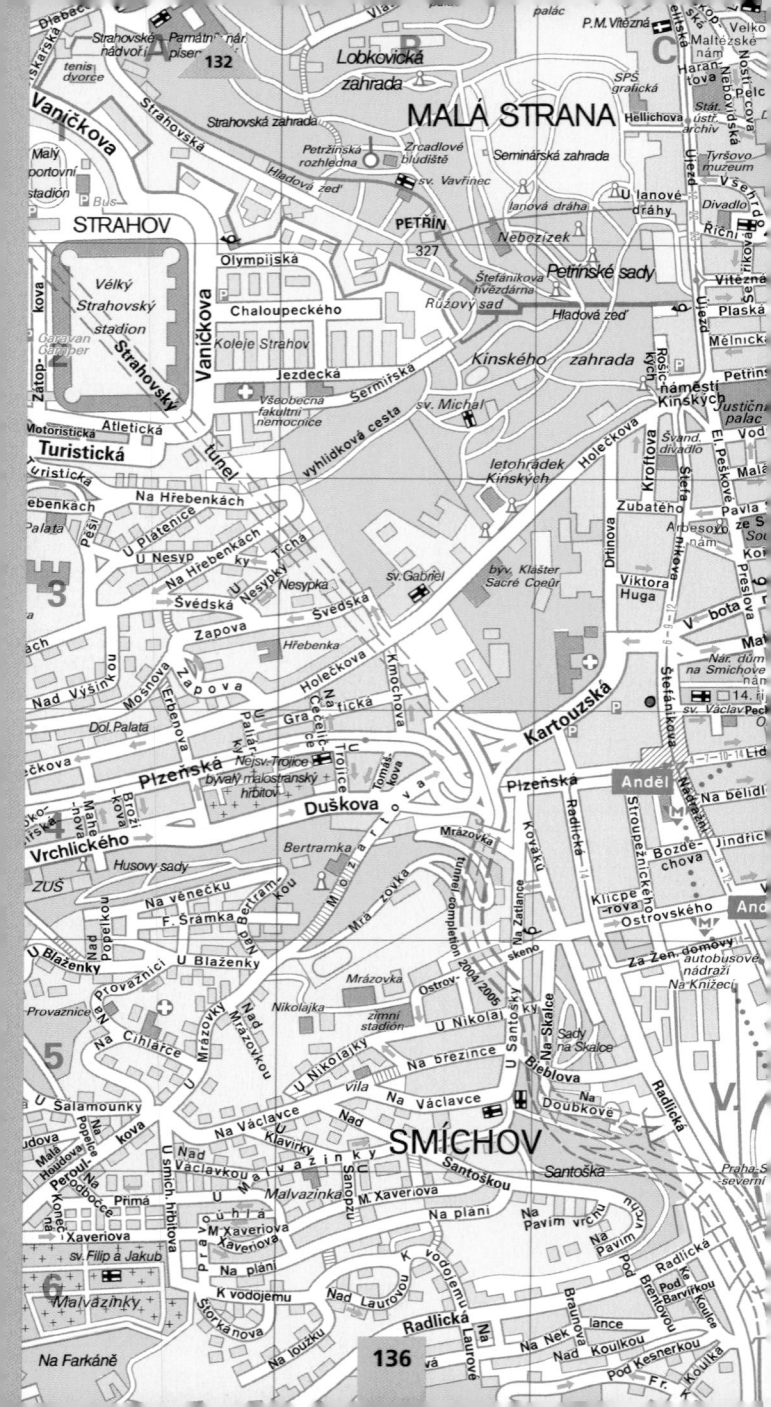

Diebac...
Strahovské Památ... nár.
nádvoří píser 132

Strahovská zahrada

LOBKOVICKÁ
zahrada

MALÁ STRANA

P.M. Vítězná

Malé
sportovní
stadión

STRAHOV

Petřínská
rozhledna

Zrcadlové
bludiště
sv. Vavřinec

Seminářská zahrada

SPŠ
grafická

Hellichova

Stát.
ústř.
archiv

Tyršovo
muzeum

Hladová zeď

Olympijská

PETŘÍN

lanová dráha

327

U lanové
dráhy

Divadlo

Řičn...

Nebozízek

Vaníčkova

Velký
Strahovský
stadión

Chaloupeckého

Koleje Strahov

Štefánikova
hvězdárna
Růžový sad

Petřínské sady

Vítězné

Plaská

Hladová zeď

Mělnick...

Caravan
Camper

Strahovský

Jezdecká

Šermířská

Kinského zahrada

náměstí
Kinského

Petřín...

Justičn...
palac

Motoristická

Všeobecná
fakultní
nemocnice

sv. Michal

Turistická

Atletická

vyhlídková cesta

letohrádek
Kinských

Holečkova

Švand.
divadlo

Krotľová

m. Peškov...

Vod...

Malá

Turistická

ebeňkách

Na Hřebenkách

U Platenice

Drtinova

Zubatého

Pavla

ze S

Sou...

Palata

Pěší

Na Hřebenkách

Nesypka

Tichá

Nesypky

Arbesovo

nám.

Koľ...

Švédská

Na Výšin...

Švédská

sv. Gabriel

býv. Klášter
Sacré Coeur

Viktora
Huga

Presľav...

...bota

Zapova

Hřebenka

... čkova

Mošnova

Zapova

Ebenova

Holečkova

Kmochova

Ma...

Nár. dům
na Smíchově
nám...

Nad Výšin...

Kartouzská

14. ...
sv. Václav Pech...

Dol. Palata

palac...

Grafická

Nejsv.-Trojice

Plzeňská

Tomáš...
kova

Anděl

Lid...

Plzeňská

Na bělidl...

...čkova

bývalý malostranský
hřbitov

Duškova

Bertramka

Mrázovka

Radlická

Stroupežnicko...

Bozdě-
chova

Jindřic...

Vrchlického

Husovy sady

Na věnečku

F. Šrámka

tunel completion
2004 2005

Klíč... ...
...rova

Ostrovského

Anď

ZUŠ

U Blaženky

Na Zatlanku

Za Žen. domovy
autobusové
nádraží

Provaznice

U Blaženky

Mrázovka

Nikolajka

zimní
stadión

Ostrov...

sken...

Na Knížecí

Salamounky

Na Cihlářce

U Mrázovky

U Nikolajky

U Nikolaj...

U Santošky

Na Skalce

Sady
na Skalce

Radlická

vila

Na březince

Bieblova

V.

...udova
Holdovsk...
Na
Perou...

Na
Popelce
Pod...

Klavírky

Nad Václavce

Na Václavce

Na
Doubkově

Praha-S
severní

Malvazinky

M. Xaveriova

Na pláni

Na
Pavím vrchu

Xaveriova

Xaveriova

Na Pavím

Přímá

Klamovka

M. Xaveriova

sv. Filip a Jakub

Na pláni

K vodojemu

Nad Laurovou

Pod
Barvírkou

Koulka

Malvazinky

Šťakanova

Radlická

...lance

Nek...

Nad Koulkou

Pod Kesnerkou

Na Farkáně

Na loučce

136

Fr. Koulk...

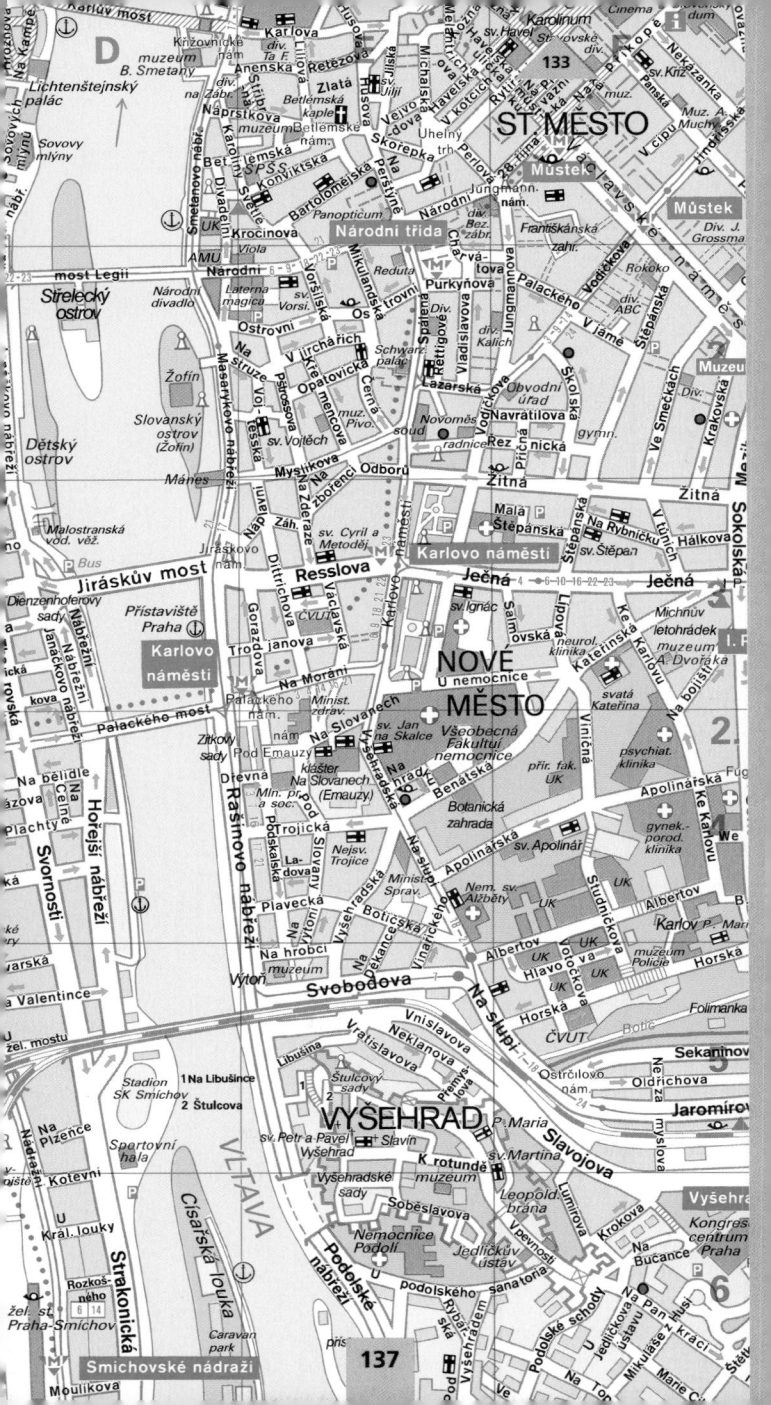

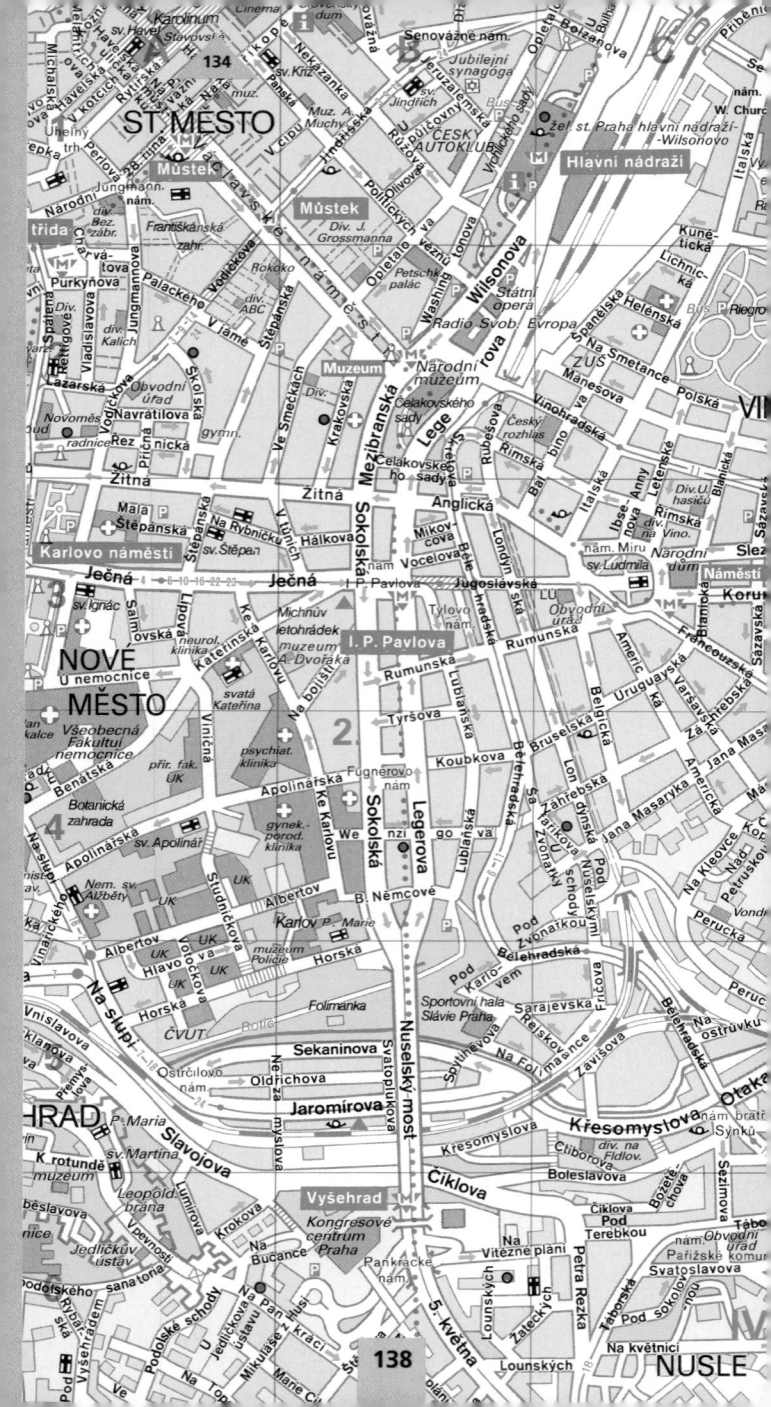

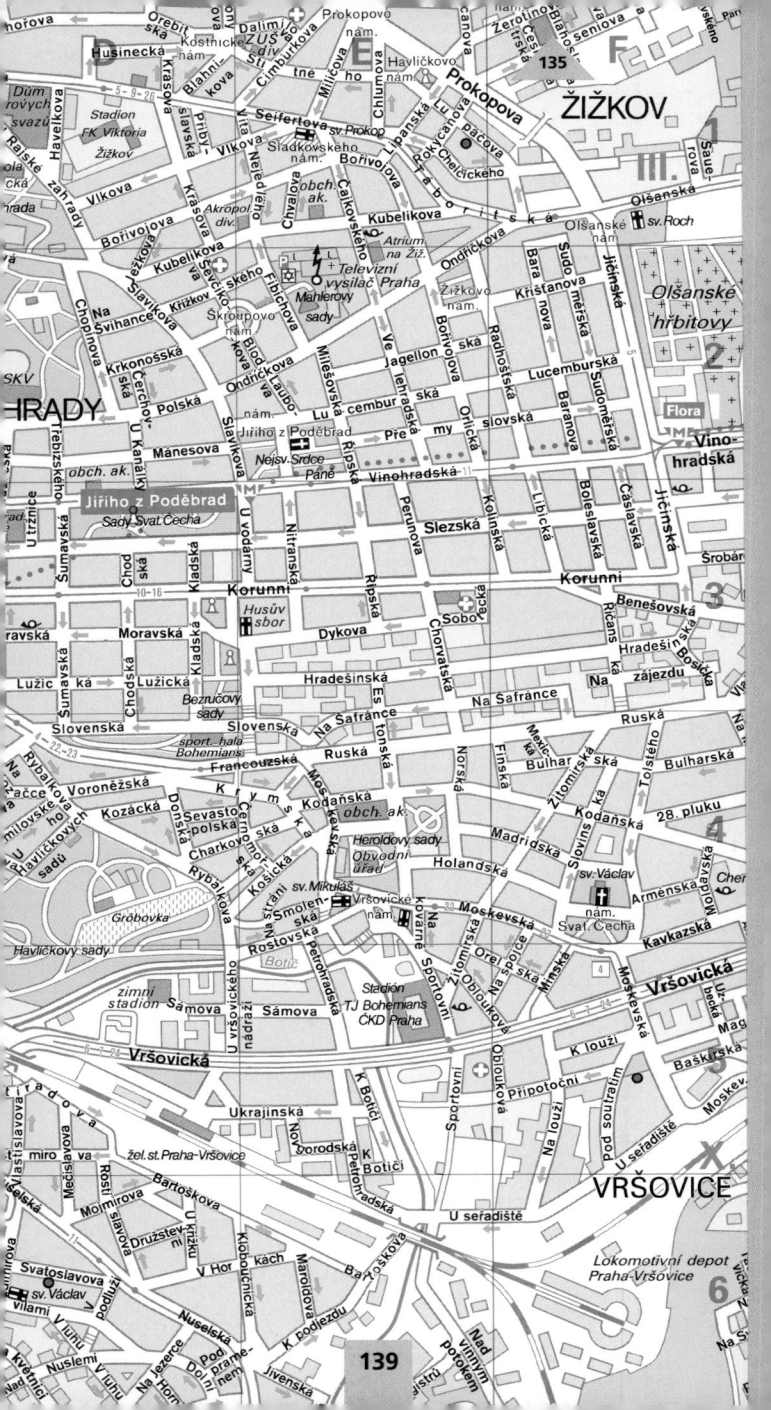

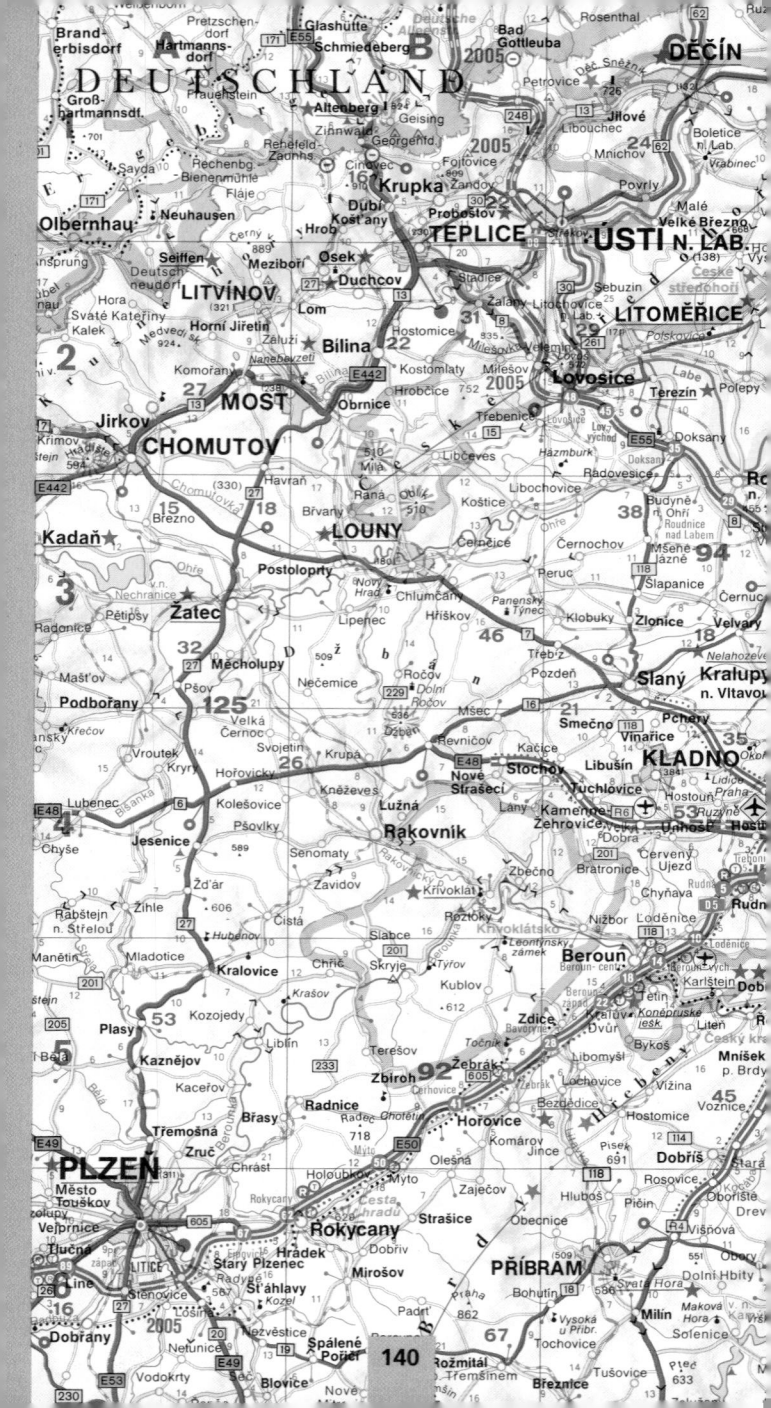

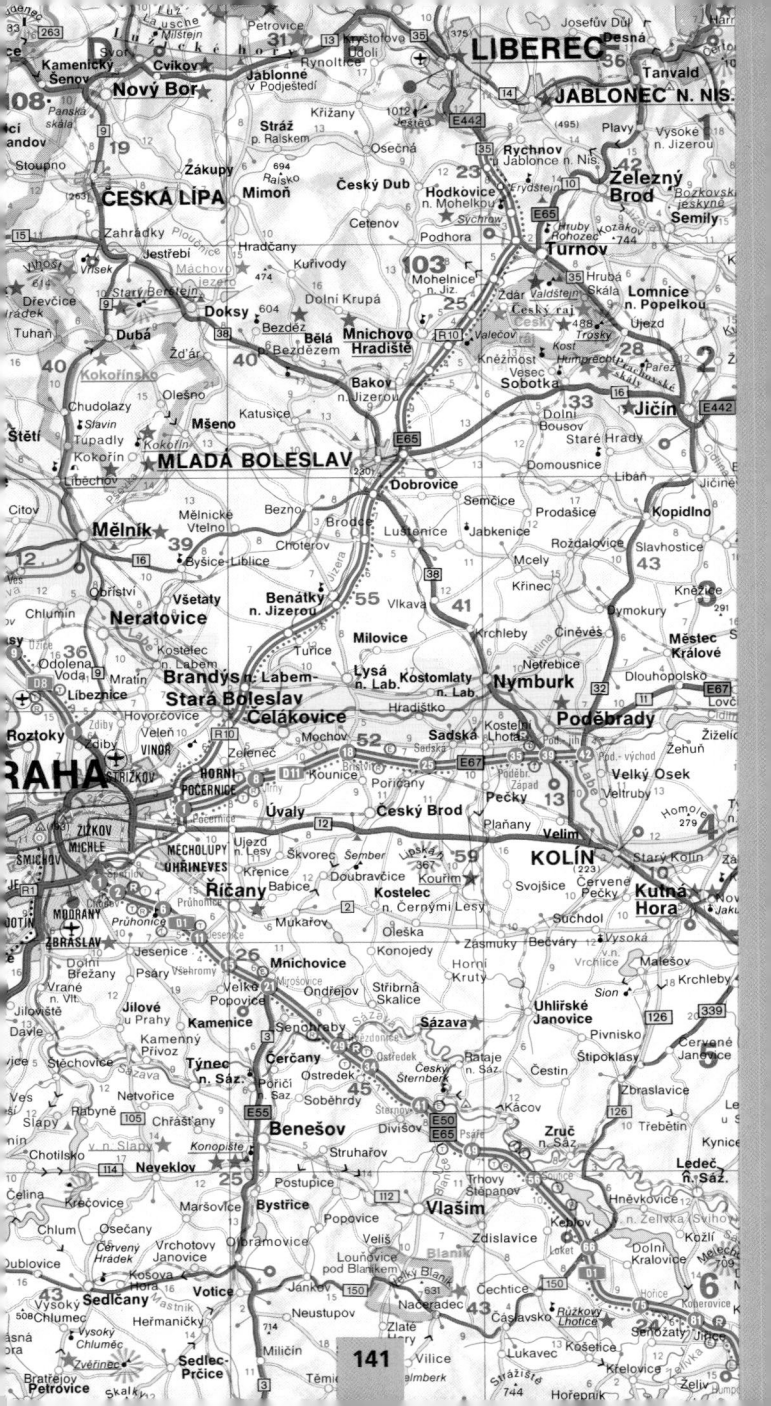

141

STREET INDEX